Unleash the Master Therapist Within

Out-of-body experiences (OBEs) at once reveal the true nature and greatest possibilities of our being. You can travel to a dimension where the effects of aging, injury, disappointment, and depression are replaced by the best the universe has to offer. A place where the painful residue of past-life issues is wiped clean. Through astral projection, anxieties associated with past-life trauma, empowerment issues, and ill health are effectively eliminated. You will finally discover new meaning to your existence as a conscious, enduring energy force in the universe.

Astral Projection and Psychic Empowerment presents several highly effective step-by-step OBE strategies developed in the lab and tested under stringently controlled conditions. The result is a comprehensive set of procedures and exercises designed to help you explore the highest realms of cosmic power and enlightenment.

You already possess the tools to unleash the master therapist within. Explore the out-of-body state and penetrate the shroud of mystery surrounding this empowering experience.

About the Author

Joe H. Slate, Ph.D. (Alabama), is a licensed psychologist in private practice. His extensive academic background led to his pioneering research on altered states and psychic processes. He is the author of *Psychic Empowerment* and *Psychic Empowerment for Health and Fitness*.

To Write to the Author

If you wish to contact the author, or would like more information about this book, please write to the author in care of Llewellyn Worldwide, and we will forward your request. Both the author and the publisher appreciate hearing from you and learning of your enjoyment of this book and how it has helped you. Llewellyn Worldwide cannot guarantee that every letter written to the author can be answered, but all will be forwarded. Please write to:

Joe H. Slate
c/o Llewellyn Worldwide
P.O. Box 64383, Dept. K636-X
St. Paul, MN 55164-0383, U.S.A.

Please enclose a self-addressed, stamped envelope for reply, or $1.00 to cover costs. If outside the U.S.A., enclose international postal reply coupon.

ASTRAL
PROJECTION
AND
PSYCHIC
EMPOWERMENT

**Techniques for Mastering
the Out-of-Body Experience**

Joe H. Slate, Ph.D.

1998
Llewellyn Publications
St. Paul, Minnesota 55164-0383 U.S.A.

FIRST EDITION
First Printing, 1998

Cover design: Tom Grewe
Book design and layout: Michael Maupin
Editing and proofreading: Rose Brandt
Photographs courtesy of Joe H. Slate

Library of Congress Cataloging-in-Publication Data
Slate, Joe H.
    Astral projection and psychic empowerment : techniques for mastering the out-of-body experience / Joe H. Slate. -- 1st ed.
        p.   cm.
    Includes index.
    ISBN 1-56718-636-X (pbk.)
    1. Astral projection.   I. Title
BF1389.A7S54   1998
133.9'5--dc21   97-48976
                                            CIP

Llewellyn Worldwide does not participate in, endorse, or have any authority or responsibility concerning private business transactions between our authors and the public.
    All mail addressed to the author is forwarded but the publisher cannot, unless specifically instructed by the author, give out an address or phone number.

Llewellyn Publications
A Division of Llewellyn Worldwide, Ltd.
P. O. Box 64383, Dept. K636-X
St. Paul, MN 55164-0383, U.S.A.

Acknowledgments

To the many people who contributed to the production of this book and to the research efforts that preceded it, I wish to express my heartfelt thanks. I am especially grateful to the scores of students who enthusiastically shared their valuable time, energies, and experiences during the course of this project. To the research subjects who not only went the second mile, but the third, fourth, and more, I will be forever indebted. Many of them participated in OBE studies that spanned their college careers, and following their graduation, some of them continued to contribute to our probes of this challenging topic.

I am enormously indebted to my learned colleagues who were collaborators, advisors, and critics for the duration of this project. We shared many hours, sometimes into the late evenings around a fireplace, in stimulating conversation. They hold my highest admiration and respect. Without their support, this book could not have been written.

Finally, to all the men and women at Llewellyn Publications, I owe an enormous debt of gratitude. Their interest in my work, and their continuous encouragement, have made this effort one of the most enjoyable and rewarding experiences of my life.

Other Books by Joe H. Slate

Contents

Introduction

The spirit is the true self, not that physical figure
that can be pointed out by your finger.

Cicero

I N OUR LONG quest for enlightenment, a good deal of ink has been spilt over questions of origins, reality, relevance, and destiny. These ancient concerns continue in our present search for knowledge, with each new discovery challenging the imagination and inspiring a deeper probe of the vast unknown. Biology and physics, emboldened by breakthrough discoveries about the origins of life in the universe, continue to uncover startling realities, many of which are invisible to the eye and, in some instances, contrary to common sense. The humanities and social sciences, prodded by unsettling global problems such as violence and bigotry, suicide and substance abuse, have sharpened their focus on solutions to the human dilemma of hopelessness, intolerance, irrelevance, and despair. Faced with infectious epidemics for which there are currently no vaccines and no cures, modern medical science has redoubled its efforts to find new treatment approaches, to include bold, innovative practices that do not discount the healing power of the mind and spirit. At the center of these compelling issues are many amazing psychic advancements that challenge us to redefine our conventional ideas, expand our search for empowering new realities, and develop alternative ways of exploring the unknown—in other words, to reinvent the paradigm of our existence.

Notwithstanding the remarkable scientific and psychic advancements of recent years, our deepest probes into the unknown have barely tinkered with the ragged edge of reality. For example, when we scan the heavens, even with our most powerful telescopes, we see but a splinter of the cosmos. Only recently have scientists discovered within that small fragment the existence of planets in other star systems. Even on our own planet, the unknown far exceeds the known. Biologists can, for instance, identify only about 10 percent of the animal life found in a given sample of deep sea mud. Despite their recent discovery of sub-atomic building blocks called *quarks*, physicists admit they may not have yet discovered a most fundamental reality—the smallest particle of matter. Perhaps even more important, a vast reserve of rich potential within our own being remains not only untapped, but largely unknown to us. A major focus of this book is innovative strategies that reach beyond the limited perspectives and procedures of conventional science.

Among the most promising psychic empowerment strategies for probing the unknown are those that involve *out-of-body experiences* (OBEs). To understand ourselves and the universe, we must exceed the limits of our cranial powers. OBEs are states of awareness in which our extra-biological element—a conscious, intelligent entity, typically called the *astral body*—temporarily disengages from the physical body. During that transient state, we are empowered to experience reality from outside the biological body, while remaining linked to it.

OBEs are at once the newest and oldest forms of space travel known. They are the newest in that only recently have we developed an *OBEs technology* that empowers us to travel voluntarily out of body to specified destinations, and initiate empowering out-of-body interactions. They are also the oldest in that many ancient cultures recognized and accepted the out-of-body phenomenon as a normal part of daily life. These cultures often incorporated OBEs into their cultural rites, and many of them anticipated the survival of consciousness following the final liberation of the spirit from the physical body at death.

The striking similarities throughout history among ancient cultures located at distant points on the planet could be explained as a product of out-of-body interactions. Although these cultures had no physical contact with each other, they almost certainly interacted psychically, and through their out-of-body visits, they could have exchanged information and acquired knowledge that produced cross-cultural similarities in values, beliefs, ceremonial rituals, and customs. Likewise, certain global trends in architectural design, particularly the pyramid, could have been shaped by out-of-body contacts, either between cultures, or on a higher common plane.

The potential range of the out-of-body experience is unlimited—it is at once both sweeping and focused. OBEs can consist simply of spontaneous out-of-body observations of familiar settings or interactions with known persons; or they can be complex gateways to distant astral planes and dimensions that are difficult to define because they exist outside the realm of material reality and seem to have no defined limits. OBEs can deliberately access a designated earth location for a specific purpose, or they can literally span the universe, including planets of other star systems. They can include empowering interactions, brilliant new insights, and spectacular quicksilver views of astral realities that challenge us mentally and spiritually. But on the average, OBEs involve ordinary, everyday life circumstances and interactions that are, nevertheless, purposeful, enriching, and empowerment driven.

Amazing as it may seem, our mental capacities during the out-of-body state are more than simply maintained; they are at once both enlarged and enriched. Supportive of that seemingly incredulous notion is the fact that many major advancements throughout the history of civilization involved mental states that clearly fit the known dynamics of OBEs. Through the centuries, crucial scientific discoveries have often been the products of mental imagery, dreams, intuitive thinking, and peak experiences, all having the fingerprints of the out-of-body state, which elevate consciousness to a higher plane of understanding.

During the typical out-of-body state, intelligence is heightened, consciousness is expanded, sensations are more vivid, and perceptions are more accurate and detailed. Typically, human experience is limited by our biological nature and the physical environment within which we function. Cognitively, we perform within the narrow limits of our genetic make-up and the confines of our environment. Normal sensation and perception are similarly limited—we consciously respond only to sensory stimulus within our sensory thresholds, and we actively attend to and perceive only a small portion of our total perceptual field. Through the out-of-body experience, we can literally transcend the biological and environmental constrictions that limit our growth and separate us from the larger realities of our existence.

OBEs often reveal new conceptual realities that go far deeper than the surface of things. Although as human beings we subconsciously understand many of the basic principles of the universe, we have to work at uncovering them. OBEs offer a magnificent vehicle for tapping into the inner sources of knowledge while probing the outer reaches of the cosmos. The result is a better understanding of cosmic principles, along with greater power in applying them to enrich our lives and to develop our full potential as human beings.

Contrary to conventional thought, many of our higher creative processes function best in the absence of a constricting biological base. The masterpieces of great artists, poets, and musicians often suggest out-of-body interactions, possibly with higher astral planes, as sources of knowledge and creative expression. For example, the poems of Edna St. Vincent Millay frequently depict images that are almost certainly of out-of-body origin, as brilliantly illustrated in her early poem, "Renascence:"

> I saw and heard, and knew at last
> The How and Why of all things, past,
> And present and forevermore.
> The universe, cleft to the core,
> Lay open to my probing sense...

Similarly, the works of many masterful artists strongly suggest OBEs as sources of creative ideas. For instance, primitive art created abstract structures with many elements of possible astral origin. Early architecture and sculpture, in particular, organized highly complex concepts into innovative designs with strong indications of astral influence. Later, the works of the many impressionists, even when viewed with a skeptical eye, reveal a conceptual and abstract style suggesting strong ethereal origins.

Although OBEs have at times been over-dramatized, romanticized, and even trivialized, they have never been more relevant to our personal growth and empowerment than today. Under the economic, social, political, and psychological pressures of modern life, the cascade of overwhelming life events can reverberate throughout our lives, generate debilitating stress, undermine our social relationships, pull friends and family apart, and lead to hopelessness and despair. OBEs can unleash abundant resources from within ourselves while connecting us to the highest sources of cosmic power. They can expand our vision, and help us see the growth opportunities that surround us. They can give us a forceful emotional and motivational lift, prepare us for action, and inoculate us against setbacks. They can teach us self-preservation, even under the most adverse circumstances. They can inspire us to press forward with determination, even in the face of fierce opposition. They can help us cope with stress, solve problems, develop positive social relationships, and succeed in achieving our loftiest goals.

Perhaps more than any other human experience, OBEs mirror the divine nature of our being as a conscious, indestructible entity. In the out-of-body state, we are compelled to experience the advanced, spiritual side of our existence. OBEs give us a powerful sense of our identity and an unwavering faith in our future. They lift the spirit to new levels of insight and power. They help us to know ourselves and the universe in ways that point to new meaning and a new vision.

From the psychic empowerment perspective, the terms *astral body, soul, spirit, higher self, non-biological being, consciousness,* and *superconsciousness* are often used interchangeably. Each can be seen, not as simply an attribute or possession of the person, but rather as the person. The psychic empowerment perspective recognizes the spiritual nature of our being. Rather than merely possessing an astral body, soul, spirit, self, or consciousness, we are all of these and more. Our *individuality, personhood,* and *identity* are permanently and inextricably linked to our total being, yet they are forever evolving. Tending to that amazing evolution and realizing our highest potentials are among the major purposes of our existence on this planet.

In summary, OBEs, possibly more than any other human experience, manifest at once the true nature and highest possibilities of our being. They reveal the divinity of our personhood and our capacity for oneness with all creation. They affirm our immortality and the certainty of our endless growth. They celebrate our existence—past, present, and future—and the purposefulness of our lives. They uncover the boundless possibilities within ourselves and the unlimited opportunities around us. Perhaps most important of all, they avow the dignity and incomparable worth of all human beings.

In the pages that follow, we will explore the out-of-body experience and its capacity to enrich and empower our lives. My major goal in writing this book is threefold: to uncover new possibilities for our personal growth and fulfillment; to develop practical, sensible, tested strategies for tapping into the inner and outer sources of wisdom and power; and lastly, to promote a new paradigm that reveals the beauty and power of our existence as a permanent life force in the cosmos. It is hoped that this book will inspire each of us to live with greater purpose and joy, both now and in the future.

1

....

The Nature of OBEs

*There is one spectacle grander than the sea, that is
the sky; there is one spectacle grander than the sky,
that is the interior of the soul.*

Victor Hugo, *Les Miserables*

THERE IS PROBABLY no other human phenomenon so steeped in mystery,
yet so potentially empowering, as the out-of-body experience. In the
out-of-body state, consciousness is liberated with incredible power to
explore itself along with other dimensions, including many wondrous
astral or spiritual planes not commonly known to us. To experience this
remarkable phenomenon is to discover new meaning to our existence as a
conscious, enduring energy force in the universe.

Out-of-body experiences (OBEs), also known as *soul travel* and *astral
projection*, are phenomena in which the non-physical or astral body literally disengages from the physical body and, in that temporary etheric
state, consciously experiences other physical realities or distant astral
planes. These out-of-body ventures of consciousness are important to our
growth because they can part the clouds that obscure our vision and limit
our awareness as human beings. OBEs, while affirming the duality of our
incarnate existence as both biological and non-biological, dissolve the
screens that often distort our perceptions and thwart our discovery of new
knowledge. They transcend the shadowy sphere of our physical world to

1

unveil brilliant new domains of power that can be tapped into. Equally as important, the out-of-body state, in liberating consciousness to soar, can unlock the door to our innermost being, uncover new growth possibilities, and lift consciousness to new heights of understanding and power. Possibly the highest source of personal empowerment, and the best clue to the meaning of our existence in the universe, lies at the door of consciousness itself.

Personal consciousness is both a *product* and a *process*. As a product, it can be seen as the astral embodiment of a unique *astral genotype,* or cosmic genetic code, which represents the permanent structure underlying our individuality as a conscious entity. In the incarnate state, consciousness with its cosmic code co-exists with the physical body and its *biological genotype* or physical genetic code. In that sense, our astral genotype as embodied in consciousness is analogous to our biological genotype as embodied in physiology. However, each lifetime of incarnation—or consciousness embodied in physiology—can be seen as only one of many possible unions, with each union or incarnation representing a single instance of the unlimited possibilities for a given cosmic code.

From a purely spiritual perspective, consciousness can be seen as the product of the indestructible essence of the soul, with its own spiritual genesis and its own unique spiritual identity. The physical body, including the brain, exists as simply a temporary, corporeal temple of the infinite spirit, a view endorsed by Pascal, who observed in 1670, "Our soul is cast into a body, where it finds number, time, and dimension." From this perspective, the ultimate goal of body/soul interaction is spiritual growth, service to humankind, and personal fulfillment, even when brain functions fail and body parts wear out. As an old Nigerian proverb says, "However broken down is the spirit's shrine, the spirit is there all the same."

As a process, personal consciousness is an ongoing, evolutionary phenomenon, in which our feelings, perceptions, and thoughts are in a state of constant interaction. Awareness of that interaction and our capacity to voluntarily intervene and direct it is essential to our self-discovery and growth. A major goal of OBEs is to lift and empower consciousness to generate new, positive interactions within the self.

An integral part of personal consciousness is that vast region commonly known as the *subconscious*, a storehouse of all experiences and potentials not currently available to conscious awareness. When consciousness is raised and empowered, we become increasingly aware of important past experiences that were somehow lost, as well as our dormant growth potentials and the abundance of inner resources available to us. But lifting consciousness to new levels must result in more than enlightenment or self-awareness. It must spawn a firm commitment and concentrated effort to develop our potentials to their peaks, while contributing to global needs and raising global consciousness. *Progressively raising personal and global consciousness to new levels of enlightenment and responsible action is the finest attitude of human expression.* OBEs, possibly more than any other human phenomenon, actively accelerates that vital process.

As a dynamic storehouse of all that has happened to us, consciousness is a complete and accurate archive of the way our lives unfold and evolve from level to level, and from the reincarnation perspective, from life to life. It is impossible, however, to precisely define consciousness and constrict it to comfortable limits—perhaps if it could be defined and constricted, it could not exist. At best, we can contemplate its fathomless nature. Consciousness is like a spattered canvas with a variety of elements—brush swipes, blobs, trickles, splats, and pigment. These elements represent only the raw tangibles of artistic expression; they do not reveal the higher creative process. The amazing capacity of consciousness to continuously grind up, blend, and transform the ingredients of experience into meaningful realities remains impenetrable.

In the out-of-body state, consciousness with its unique cosmic identity and accumulated experiences is freed of biological constraints to experience other realities. OBEs significantly expand our growth options, while manifesting the developmental and survival nature of consciousness as independent of biology. From a spiritual perspective, this growth phenomenon is often seen as *soul travel*, in which the soul imbued with consciousness leaves the physical body and travels to distant realities, including higher spiritual dimensions as sources of new insight and power. The Bible refers to this phenomenon in II Corinthians 12:3,4: "And I knew such a man, whether in the body, or out of the body...how that he was caught up into paradise, and heard unspeakable words..."

The capacity of personal consciousness to disengage the biological body and function independent of it can be illustrated by the metaphor of a machine and its engine, with the machine representing the biological body and its engine representing consciousness. The power produced by the engine to energize the machine and its various functions parallels the power of consciousness to energize the body and its many biological processes, including the complex activities of the brain. Just as the engine is the driving force of the machine, consciousness is the driving force of the physical body. When separate from the machine, the disengaged engine retains its independent capacity for power. This phenomenon parallels the out-of-body state, in which consciousness, although disengaged from the physical body, retains its functional powers as an independent, non-biological entity.

One view of OBEs holds that the disengaged astral body remains connected to the biological body by an astral energy component called the *silver cord*, which assures physical survival during out-of-body travel, not only to distant physical destinations but to intangible dimensions as well. The silver cord is occasionally perceived as a shimmering stream of radiant energy connecting the astral body to its physical body counterpart. The astral body is often described as an aura-like but uniquely recognizable form of bright energy. This perspective of OBEs asserts that personal consciousness and identity are imbued in the astral body. Death is seen simply as a growth transition accompanied by a severing of the silver cord and full liberation of our non-biological being. Supporting this view are the observations of health-care professionals who often report an aura-like form rising from the physical body of dying patients.

A related view of OBEs holds that as we fall asleep, the astral or etheric body spontaneously slips out of the biological body and, while linked to the corporeal body by the silver cord, remains in that disengaged state of consciousness for the duration of sleep. Certain dream-like experiences, particularly experiences of drifting over terrain or traveling in space, are believed to be astral travel. In Chapter Six, we will present step-by-step strategies designed to induce out-of-body travel during sleep.

OBEs suggest a complex interaction between the biological and non-biological dimensions of our existence. We are simply carbon-based organisms whose origin and destiny are carbon dust; but non-biologically, we are unique, conscious, intelligent entities whose origin is ethereal and whose destiny is continuous growth and permanent survival beyond death. Our biological system offers a tangible but temporary vehicle for growth—it equips us with the mechanisms required to engage our physical environment and interact with it. Included in that physical vehicle are the functions of the central nervous system and our basic physiological drives, such as hunger, thirst, sex, activity, and sleep—all designed to sustain our existence and facilitate our growth in this tangible reality. Typically, our basic physical needs must be fulfilled before we can focus effectively on our higher consciousness needs, including our psychic development and spiritual actualization.

Although our biological functions are critical to our physical survival, at times achieving our loftiest goals requires postponement of physical gratification, forfeiture of material interests, and in some instances, even risk to our personal well-being. Paradoxically, adversity and misfortune often provide the seminal conditions for our spiritual actualization and on a larger scale, our cultural advancement. As Heraclitus noted in 500 B.C., "Greater dooms win greater destinies." When higher consciousness intervenes, even our physical survival can become secondary to our altruistic strivings, such as personal dignity, human rights, and freedom. A firm commitment to a noble cause can eclipse even our most basic temporal needs. We may, for instance, sacrifice our lives for freedom or chose death over enslavement. Likewise, an unwavering set of moral values can be a critical guide that regulates our mental, physical, and social conduct, even in the face of catastrophic, life-threatening events. We may, for instance, take extreme risks to our personal safety to rescue victims of a disaster or come to the aid of an animal in distress. The fact that our physical drives are often secondary to our non-physical strivings suggests a complex alliance in which consciousness and its strivings often transcend physiology and its needs.

Further reflecting the complex nature of our being are the ongoing interactions between consciousness and physiology, many of which demonstrate the power of the mind over the body. Illustrating that phenomenon are recent medical studies showing that prayer, whether offered for oneself or for another, significantly promotes physical healing. Also, a sense of humor has been found to enhance our physical as well as mental well-being. One of the most powerful health and fitness tools known is our capacity to deliberately initiate empowering experiences within the self. We can, for instance, intentionally generate positive mental states that alter brain-wave patterns, forge new neural connections, repair damaged tissue, and even slow the aging process. Conversely, negative emotions and a pessimistic, disempowering attitude invariably exact a severe toll on our total being. Whether empowering or disempowering, these experiences within the self clearly illustrate the remarkable capacity of consciousness to independently alter both mental and physical functions.

One of the most direct manifestations of the sheer power of consciousness is *psychokinesis* (PK), the human capacity to influence matter or motion independently of physical force. Whether it is used to directly influence matter, including inner biological functions, or to induce motion in an external object, PK offers further evidence not only of our dual nature, but also of the distinct dominance of mental functions over the physical body. Perhaps nowhere is that dominance more objectively illustrated than in the use of biofeedback. In a carefully controlled laboratory situation, biofeedback instruments can precisely record our physiological responses to various non-physical stimuli such as mental imagery and suggestion. Among the commonly observed responses are changes in heart rate, blood pressure, body temperature, galvanic skin response, and brain-wave pattern. Our power to consciously intervene in the so-called "autonomic" biological functions, including the neural activity of the brain, and to independently engage the physical body in a healthful interaction suggests a host of important treatment possibilities in the clinical setting, particularly for stress-related disorders. PK power is but another example of the supremacy of consciousness and the exciting possibilities of sheer mind power.

In hypnosis and self-hypnosis, along with certain meditation states, we see further evidence of our dual makeup and the powerful role of consciousness over physiology. Hypnotic suggestions as instruments of consciousness are often designed to elicit highly specific physical sensations, including those required to deepen the trance state. On the other hand, they can be designed to initiate new, highly complex physical response patterns, such as those required to reduce physical tension, control pain, and fortify the immune system. In each instance, the power of consciousness to produce a desired biological effect provides another example of the complex physical/non-physical interaction of our temporal existence in this earthly dimension.

If through interactive strategies such as biofeedback, hypnosis, and meditation we can *deliberately engage* the physical body to independently alter existing functions and initiate new ones, including those of the brain, it would logically follow that we could deliberately disengage from the physical body and, in that disengaged state, function independent of physiology. This simple premise provides a reasonable rationale for OBEs as a growth and discovery phenomenon, not as an illusion or leap of imagination. In the final analysis, out-of-body travel and our relentless search for meaning point inexorably to a logical conclusion: *Biology is not destiny, but rather a transient vehicle for spiritual growth and discovery on this physical plane.*

Like sleep, the hypnotic trance state often sets the stage for spontaneous out-of-body travel. It's not surprising then, that trance procedures, as described later in this book, can be purposefully structured to facilitate an easy disengagement of consciousness from the physical body, and initiate out-of-body travel for specific growth purposes. But even in the absence of a structured procedure or intent to produce the experience, many trance subjects, although untrained in out-of-body travel, will slip effortlessly out of body during the hypnotic state.

In the out-of-body state, the interaction between consciousness and physiology occurs more indirectly, but with increased empowerment potential. As the physical body remains at rest, consciousness is liberated to engage itself with the highest sources of power. In that out-of-body state, positive, healthful energies can be generated and readily transmitted to influence physical functions. At a more advanced level, OBEs can tap into higher astral planes to access new sources of knowledge, healing, and power. A major goal of many OBEs is to generate a more positive, empowering interaction between the self and higher astral planes.

The complex nature of our being and our capacity to disengage the physical body raise important questions regarding the nature of personal consciousness and identity. Our existence and the unique makeup of our individuality are explained as simply the products of heredity and environment. The *nature versus nurture* controversy continues to speculate on the influence of these forces. Often missing from the equation, however, is the power of the *conscious self* to choose and determine its own evolution. The single most important regulating force in our growth and evolution as human beings is personal choice. The quality of our lives in the present and the future is shaped by choice, not by chance or some pre-determined destiny.

OBEs are a reflection of the energizing, indestructible life force underlying our existence. That powerful unifying force transcends all the influences of biology, culture, and environment. It is the *essence of our existence as a conscious entity*. In the out-of-body state, we experience that essence in its full splendor and glory.

The richness of the out-of-body state is characterized by a liberation of personal consciousness that can illuminate our lives and expand our awareness of other realities—from the nearest physical location to the most distant celestial plane. OBEs can be as simple and spontaneous as a brief wandering beyond the body, or as complex and deliberate as an interaction with the highest dimensions of unlimited power.

In the out-of-body state, our awareness shifts outward as we experience our existence externally to, and independently of, our physical body. Our perceptions typically become more vivid and detailed. Cognitive abilities, such as creativity, memory, and problem-solving, often reach their peaks. Our language limitations are usually exceeded, and our capacity for pleasure and social interaction is enriched in a shifted state of awareness.

Many spontaneous OBEs seem to specifically lift personal awareness to a new level. All too often, we live a screened existence: enslaved by apathy, thwarted by circumstances, and consequently we are unable to act. OBEs can generate new visions of possibilities by lifting the veils that dull our senses and dim our awareness. They can inspire peak moments of enlightenment, attune us to the universe, and empower us to transcend the limitations of our physical existence on this planet.

In the out-of-body state, *extrasensory perception* (ESP) is nearly always heightened. In fact, among the most effective ESP training procedures known are those that utilize OBEs to activate psychic channels and stimulate psychic growth. Psychic impressions of the future (*precognition*); psychic awareness of the past (*retrocognition*); expanded insight concerning distant, unseen realities (*clairvoyance*); and mind-to-mind communication (*telepathy*) often occur spontaneously in the out-of-body state. The out-of-body state can activate our highest psychic faculties. Not surprisingly, expanded awareness of past lifetimes frequently occurs during the astral experience.

Although clairvoyance often occurs during the out-of-body state, OBEs cannot be dismissed simply as psychic impressions of distant realities. Experienced clairvoyants who also report frequent OBEs describe the two phenomena as vastly different, both in their underlying dynamics and in the nature of the experiences themselves. Clairvoyance—the ESP of tangible objects, current happenings, and existing conditions—is a psychic faculty requiring no out-of-body travel. Out-of-body travel, on the other hand, requires a disengagement of the astral from the physical, and subsequent travel. Although the underlying dynamics of OBEs and ESP differ, the end results can be the same—expanded awareness and knowledge not otherwise available to us.

At the cutting edge of psychic science and technology are recent discoveries suggesting the amazing capacity of consciousness in the out-of-body state to simultaneously engage multiple realities, a phenomenon we call *multi-location OBEs*. The most common of these is *bi-location* or the simultaneous engagement of consciousness in two locations. Multi-location OBEs are not limited to temporal realities; they can simultaneously engage multiple astral planes and initiate multiple interactions between them. Although these complex phenomena are often explained as higher forms of clairvoyance,when they occur during the out-of-body state they meet the criteria for OBEs. This remarkable power of consciousness in the out-of-body state to simultaneously engage itself in multiple realities is called *astral span*, a phenomenon that demonstrates our ability to transcend sensory perception and engage the universe outside of sensory stimulation.

Another astounding phenomenon sometimes associated with the out-of-body state is *materialization*, which is commonly explained as an astral transformation proces, comparable to snow crystallizing from water vapor. Materialization can be seen as a tangible representation of astral energy in which thoughts, other intangibles, and in some instances distant tangibles assume a physical presence, often spontaneously. Materializations from this perspective can also include the conversion of the astral body itself into a visible energy form. Apparitions, including those collectively perceived, could be explained as the materialization of the astral energies of either discarnates or possibly, out-of-body incarnates.

From another perspective, materialization can be explained as a form of *out-of-body psychokinesis* (PK), or the psychic capacity to influence matter while in the out-of-body state. According to this view, materialization reflects the power of consciousness to literally transport and relocate material objects, as well as to amass energy and use it to produce visible representations of material objects. Out-of-body PK, however, is not limited to the external materialization process. When focused on the physical body, PK can alter physiology and create biological change. In its highest and most elegant form, out-of-body PK could either *repair* a damaged organ or literally *recreate* a new one. Conceivably, this is one of the most important, yet most neglected, health and fitness resources of our time.

The out-of-body experience cannot be dismissed simply as a fanciful illusion, or a product of our imagination. We can, of course, generate imaginative pictures of distant realities, and we can, through fantasy, interact with them. But such experiences, while potentially empowering, are products of the creative self rather than out-of-body travel. OBEs, on the other hand, are valid phenomena, in which we can both observe and actively participate in conditions at a spatial distance from the physical body.

One popular theory about OBEs involves the role of consciousness as an etheric counterpart of the biological experience in the physical world. In this concept, sometimes called the *synthesis view*, OBEs are manifestations of the pure cosmic energy that sustains our consciousness while energizing our biological existence and helping us to function in the physical domain. The energized biological system, in turn, provides a functional area for our spiritual evolution as a life-force entity. Our *biological evolution* equips us physically to adapt to the demands of temporal reality. Our *spiritual evolution*, on the other hand, is a continuous unfolding process of ascension to new levels of enlightenment and power. The result is a continuous, upward spiral of raised personal—and by extension, global—consciousness.

Our spiritual evolution, while continuous, is not always even. We experience rapid growth spurts and extraordinary quantum leaps, as well as periods of slowed growth and plateaus where our growth processes, while seemingly at rest, often position themselves for a future growth spurt. At times, a growth faculty may seem to falter or literally decline, but other faculties will forge ahead to fill in the void. OBEs are important to our development because of their capacity to energize and accelerate the growth spiral.

Our existence as a spiritual being transcends our biological limitations in both endurance and growth potential. The physical body is a magnificent creation, with complex organs, functions, and systems, all designed to work together in amazing harmony. Notwithstanding the genius of our physical design, our biological organs will eventually wear out and our physical systems will inevitably fail. Our biological destiny is physical decline and death. Our spiritual destiny, on the other hand, is permanence and continued growth. The out-of-body experience is a preview of the unlimited possibilities awaiting each of us in that liberated, enriched state beyond the gateway of death. If we retain conscious awareness of our individuality during the temporary out-of-body state, it would follow that after death and final astral disengagement from the body, conscious awareness would continue unaltered, or perhaps in even greater enlightened form. OBEs not only reaffirm our discarnate destiny, they facilitate our later transition to the other side when death leans against the door. Equally as important, they provide the important groundwork for our continued growth in the life-after-life realm of enriched existence.

OBEs reveal wonders never before imagined, including an acute awareness of higher planes and the intelligent astral entities who welcome our out-of-body visits and interactions. Through our experiences with advanced discarnates, angels, and ministering guides, our lives can be enriched and empowered with totally new growth possibilities. As Albert Einstein once wrote:

> The fairest thing we can experience is the mysterious. It is the fundamental emotion which stands at the cradle of true art and true science. He who knows it not and can no longer feel amazement is as good as dead, a snuffed-out candle.

OBEs manifest the unlimited power of human consciousness to probe itself, discover new realities, and interact with the highest of cosmic planes. Possibly more than any other human experience, OBEs reveal the permanence, beauty, and wonder of our existence by putting us in touch with our lives and helping us discover our highest spirituality.

2

Spontaneous OBEs

I only ask to be free. The butterflies are free.

Charles Dickens, *Bleak House*

A LTHOUGH THE OUT-OF-BODY state can be voluntarily induced through specially designed strategies, some of our most profound OBEs are spontaneous. The spontaneous experience requires no deliberate effort, and it typically runs its course independent of our intervention.

Like voluntarily induced OBEs, the spontaneous experience is always growth-oriented and purposeful in nature. It can be as simple as daydreaming, or as complex as the peak experience. It can expand our awareness of our surroundings, or it can connect us to totally new dimensions of knowledge and power. It can probe the innermost part of our being, or tap into the highest realms of the cosmos.

Even when they involve ordinary concerns of everyday life, spontaneous OBEs can be profoundly empowering. A psychologist, for instance, experienced a spontaneous, out-of-body visit to Cairo, Egypt a few days prior to her first business trip to that unfamiliar city. Traveling out-of-body, she entered the lobby of a Cairo hotel, where she noted an unusual red and yellow telephone at the registration desk. Although she had been apprehensive about the trip, she felt secure and confident during the out-of-body visit. Upon her arrival at the Cairo hotel a few days later, the familiar red and yellow telephone immediately commanded her attention. She felt instantly comforted by the serenity that had accompanied her out-of-body visit. She attributed the highly rewarding results of her business trip to the empowering effects of the out-of-body experience.

A graduate student reported a spontaneous out-of-body experience that gave him a winning edge in his preparation for a reading competency examination in German—one of the requirements for his doctoral degree. In the out-of-body state, he visited the scheduled examination room and saw a German textbook, from which, he assumed, the translation material for the two-hour examination would be selected. After the OBE, he immediately acquired a copy of the textbook from the university library and focused his preparation efforts on it. The following week, he successfully passed the competency examination, which consisted, as expected, of material taken from the familiar textbook. He regarded the incident an appropriate application of OBEs, in that it violated no university code of conduct. He believed, however, that deliberately using OBEs, or any other means, to surreptitiously gather highly specific course evaluation materials prior to an examination would raise serious ethical questions.

Spontaneous OBEs often relate to crucial personal issues, such as important career decisions. Along that line, a law student experienced a series of OBEs that seemed to pave the way for his future affiliation with a prestigious law firm. In the out-of-body visits, he entered the building where the firm's offices were located, observed the firm's work in progress, and viewed the exact office he would later occupy. These frequent visits oriented him to the firm's activities and crystallized his plans to join the firm. He began to see his affiliation with the firm as his career destiny. Upon completing his law degree, he was the firm's first choice from a long list of applicants. The out-of-body visits generated a self-fulfilling expectancy effect, empowering him to shape his future with the firm as a highly successful trial attorney.

Along another line, spontaneous OBEs are often related to therapy and health issues. They are, in fact, among our most effective therapeutic tools. Through the out-of-body state, we can become more finely attuned to the master therapist within each of us. Therapeutic insight often emerges during the out-of-body state. Disturbed and painful relationships are seen in a different light. Distressing problems seem less catastrophic, and we begin to see the light at the end of the tunnel. We discover more effective and creative ways of working through the various layers of complicated conflicts and promoting personal reintegration.

Expanding the therapeutic possibilities of spontaneous OBEs are the abundant resources of higher astral planes. The empowering effects of higher plane interventions can be profound and enduring. Spontaneous recoveries from life-threatening illnesses, the life-changing effects of the near-death experience, and the intensely empowering consequences of the peak experience are some examples. Although the mental and physical healing powers of higher planes have long been recognized, only recently have we developed the technology required to deliberately tap into their abundant resources, including the healing powers of higher plane entities, such as caring angels and guides. Awareness of guardian angels and ministering guides alone is therapeutic, but experiencing their direct intervention in our lives and interacting with them are among the most powerful healing phenomena known.

Perhaps nowhere is the therapeutic power of spontaneous OBEs more evident than when we are confronted with adversity and loss. A mother whose hospitalized child lay near death in an irreversible coma, experienced a spontaneous out-of-body interaction that allowed her to face with courage the most painful experience of her life. Kneeling in the hospital's chapel, she sensed the unmistakable presence of a comforting astral guide. Taking her by the hand, the guide gently lifted her from her body and led her away to a bright dimension of indescribable beauty. There she was surrounded by caring angels who gave her comfort and strength. She was then gently escorted back to her body by the astral guide. The serenity of the experience lingered, and helped prepare her for the loss of her child a few days later. Soon after the child's transition, she again traveled spontaneously out-of-body, this time during sleep, to a beautiful garden where she saw from a distance the familiar angels, lovingly watching over her child happily at play with other children. Instantly, she felt wonderful peace as the pain of her loss lifted.

In times of critical illness, spontaneous OBEs can foster healing, both mentally and physically. Following a two-year battle with a serious respiratory disorder, a teacher spontaneously experienced an unforgettable out-of-body encounter, which permanently affected her life. Here is her report:

> While resting in my bedroom on a rainy afternoon, I suddenly felt very light and free, as if I could go anywhere or do anything. I was then enveloped in a warm, glowing mist that seemed to soak deep inside and lift me gently away from my body. Suspended over my body, I heard an echo-like voice assuring me that I was protected and loved. Everything suddenly turned white like clouds, and I knew with certainty that I was experiencing the other side of life. Lingering momentarily in that suspended state, I felt only pure love. I then gently returned to my body. All fear of death had vanished, and my total outlook on life had changed.

Amazingly, the unforgettable out-of-body encounter not only resulted in a rapid recovery from her illness, it also initiated a period of accelerated growth and gave new meaning to her life.

Spontaneous OBEs are frequently provoked by critical life-and-death situations. A businesswoman recalls a near-death experience, during which she was accompanied to the other side by a band of caring angels. The experience occurred at a vacation resort when she went swimming alone late at night. An inexperienced swimmer, she inadvertently ventured beyond the safe swimming zone and was drawn by the current into deeper waters. Her futile efforts to return to shore resulted in panic and overpowering fatigue. Finally she stopped fighting, and immediately found herself enveloped in a brilliant light. She recalls:

> I was suddenly surrounded by a gathering of angels who, with outstretched hands, gently lifted me out of the water. I felt warm and totally secure. Soaring upward, I soon found myself in a different place, calm and unafraid. Still accompanied by angels, I recognized my father, who was reaching out to greet me. But rather than being old as I remembered him, he was at his prime, mentally and physically. The effects of the chronic illness and stroke that ended his life had vanished. I saw only youthfulness and a beaming smile. When we lovingly embraced, I sensed the joy of his transformation and the

warm glow that surrounded him. Throughout the experience, I felt no urgency or sense of time or space, only the happiness of the moment and total peace.

Soon, I was again surrounded by angels who, as before, reached out and lovingly lifted me upward. Then suddenly, I found myself at the lake, but instead of struggling, I was being drawn gently, as if by an unseen force, to the safety of shallow water, and then onto the shore. The experience empowered my life with a new vision of my destiny.

As illustrated by these examples, spontaneous OBEs can be significant sources of enlightenment and power. They can, in fact, be critical turning points in our lives. They can literally tap into the resources of higher planes to meet our most urgent needs. Our spontaneous journeys into the discarnate realm give us realistic glimpses of the other side, and manifest the transforming power of our future transition. They lift us to our highest peaks and affirm with certainty the richness of life on the other side. They reveal our future existence as the culmination of our brightest dreams and highest hopes. They uncover a dimension in which the effects of aging, illness, injury, disappointment, and oppression are replaced by the best that the universe has to offer.

3

OBEs Induction and Management Strategies

Give me somewhere to stand, and I will move the earth.

Archimedes

I F SPONTANEOUS OBEs are consistently purposeful and empowerment-driven, it would follow that the deliberately induced experience would likewise possess empowering potential, and could be equally as empowering. Out-of-body procedures have, consequently, been specifically designed to achieve a wide range of personal empowerment goals. In this chapter, we will examine several laboratory-based out-of-body induction and management strategies, with particular emphasis on procedures that promote our personal growth and development.

As already noted, spontaneous or involuntary OBEs require no deliberate effort to initiate, and they typically run their course independently of our personal intervention. Voluntary OBEs, on the other hand, are deliberately induced and managed, usually for the purpose of achieving a particular goal. Notwithstanding these differences, spontaneous and voluntary OBEs are essentially two sides of the same empowerment coin. Both are purposeful, and their underlying dynamics are essentially the same. Both require a disengagement of the astral body from its biological counterpart, and both liberate consciousness to experience realities beyond the confines of common sensory experience.

A major advantage of voluntary OBEs, aside from the fact that they can be induced at will, is their structural design and built-in capacity to achieve designated goals. To maximize their empowerment potential, voluntary OBEs require two sets of acquired strategies—induction and management. Induction strategies are designed to induce the appropriate out-of-body state, whereas management strategies are applied during the out-of-body state to direct the experience toward designated goals. Also, acquired management strategies can be used to intervene into spontaneous OBEs and direct their outcomes. Together, OBEs induction and management skills provide the essential components of an emerging OBEs technology that presents new challenges and creative options for all who wish to use this powerful tool. Like the artist who is master of the canvas, we can now become masters of the out-of-body experience.

The same conditions that influence our overall development also affect our development of OBEs skills. Among the most critical of these conditions are a willingness to take command of our lives and a strong intent to learn and grow. Other influencing factors include a positive self-concept, an open mind, and a thirst for new knowledge.

Although numerous OBEs induction and management procedures have been developed, no one best approach or set of techniques has been forthcoming. Each person is different and approaches the out-of-body experience differently, requiring variations in induction and management procedures. Furthermore, no universally accepted theory of OBEs around which to develop procedures has yet been developed. This should not surprise us, however, since no universally accepted theory of personality, psychotherapy, or even creation has yet been developed. It remains up to each of us to explore a variety of approaches in our efforts to discover those concepts and strategies that fit our needs and work best for us individually.

OBEs induction procedures are important in at least two ways: First, they offer alternative methods that consider individual differences in preferences, abilities, and needs; and as previously noted, they can be used on command to induce the optimal out-of-body state required to achieve a particular goal. We are not, therefore, required to wait for the out-of-body event to occur spontaneously; we can bring it forth at will to meet our growth and empowerment needs.

OBEs management strategies are also important in at least two ways: first, they can be applied to direct both voluntary and involuntary OBEs and focus them on specific empowerment goals; and second, they ensure productive travel while offering protection from potentially disempowering astral experiences. We are not, consequently, helpless participants in astral events that, without our intervention, could fall short or in some way be interrupted.

In developing our out-of-body skills, there can be no substitute for practice. Even experienced out-of-body travelers find that practice is essential in fine-tuning their old strategies and mastering new ones. Only through practicing various approaches can we discover those techniques that meet our personal needs and work best for us individually. Equally as important, practicing our out-of-body skills increases our awareness of ourselves and puts us in touch with our spiritual side. Through OBEs, we can discover the spiritual resources of higher astral planes. For instance, many out-of-body travelers discover their higher plane teachers, spiritual guides, and personal angels, some of whom had ministered to them from birth. With practice, the out-of-body experience can extinguish our natural fear of the unknown and replace it with optimism and joyful anticipation. Even death takes on a new perspective—it becomes an exciting passage into the light of a new and enriched existence, rather than a dreaded leap into the darkness of the unknown.

OBEs seldom have negative side-effects, but in the absence of appropriate management strategies, temporary disempowering effects have been known to occur. The most common adverse reaction seems to be associated with the fear of either losing control of the experience or failing to re-unite safely with the physical body. The possibility of any negative physical or mental effect during the experience can be minimized or extinguished altogether by appropriate induction and management strategies.

A peaceful mental state, empowering imagery, and appropriate affirmations, all designed to generate positive energy, are among the critical components in almost all OBEs empowerment procedures. Of equal, if not greater, importance is a heightened awareness of the powerful resources of higher astral planes for the duration of the out-of-body experience. Many out-of-body travelers report the spontaneous presence of a familiar ministering angel or guide who offers constant protection and guidance during the out-of-body experience. The most highly effective empowerment strategies emphasize the early invocation of higher plane protection. This can ensure the ministering presence of advanced astral entities for the duration of the out-of-body experience. These protective, energizing resources are typically invoked prior to induction and intermittently as needed throughout the experience to continually envelop one's total being—mental, physical, and spiritual—with powerful astral energy. A constant awareness of the empowering resources of higher planes is, of course, not only important to OBEs, but an integral part of every empowered life.

Certain preparatory OBEs exercises have been found useful in promoting the out-of-body state. Meditative procedures using a lighted candle, for instance, can be highly effective in developing the concentration skills required to induce and manage the experience. By focusing our attention on the candle and affirming our empowerment goals, we can also generate an mental and physical state conducive to out-of-body travel. The candle, however, is recommended primarily as a practice tool rather than an induction aid. For safety reasons, it should always be extinguished before one enters the out-of-body state.

Another excellent preparatory technique is called *Moon View*. This procedure requires comfortably focusing for a few minutes on the moon, preferably the full moon, and then, with eyes closed, imagining oneself literally visiting the moon, exploring its surface craters, planes, and caverns. In our OBEs studies, college students using this procedure often imagined visiting the unseen side of the moon. When asked to draw a map of the moon's other side following their experiences, they drew maps that were remarkably similar, a finding that suggests they may have actually traveled out-of-body to view the other side of the moon.

Another effective practice strategy developed in our laboratories is *In-Body Travel*. For this procedure, the subject selects a small body area—a hand, finger, or toe—and centers full attention on that isolated area's physical sensations. New sensations, such as warmth, numbness, tingling, and pressure are then produced and removed. Next, attention is moved from one body area to another, producing and removing sensations. The procedure is concluded by bringing all physical sensations to complete rest. While designed only as a preliminary conditioning procedure, In-Body Travel can be used to induce the out-of-body state by envisioning the astral body rising above the physical body, while the physical body remains at complete rest and free of all sensations.

Preparatory OBEs exercises often include practice in creative imagery, particularly emphasizing motion. Slow-moving clouds, a leaf in the breeze, a sail at sea, or even a magic carpet ride are good examples. The effects of these images are enhanced when they are envisioned as vehicles bearing the astral body away from the physical body and into the distance. A variation of this procedure envisions the astral body as a passenger in a transportation vehicle, such as a spacecraft, in which it can be transported to a variety of destinations.

These practice procedures exercise our mental capacity to reach beyond the confines of the biological body. By engaging imagery of a particular destination, we can further prepare ourselves mentally and physically for out-of-body travel. Aspects of each practice exercise can often be incorporated into the more comprehensive OBEs induction and management strategies, including the very highly structured, step-by-step procedures.

The typical out-of-body experience consists of four distinct steps: 1) disengagement; 2) travel; 3) destination; and 4) return. Occasionally, skilled travelers, upon inducing the out-of-body state, will give permission for the flight, destination, and return to unfold spontaneously and independently of their direct control. Nevertheless, they remain poised throughout the experience to deliberately intervene whenever necessary to re-direct the flight or to make in-flight adjustments.

The following guidelines identify the major conditions generally considered essential for successful OBEs. They provide a flexible framework within which more specific procedures can be implemented to achieve a variety of OBEs goals.

Step 1: Disengagement

The induced disengagement of the astral from the biological is typically initiated by first allowing the physical body to become deeply relaxed and then, with the eyes closed, clearing the mind of active thought. Whether in the seated or reclining position, legs should remain uncrossed so as not to cut off circulation. Hands typically rest comfortably at the sides, and in the lap for the seated or reclining position. Once the body is fully relaxed and the mind is cleared, a positive state of well-being is generated through appropriate imagery and self-empowering affirmations. Examples are:

> *I am relaxed and at complete peace with myself and the universe. I am surrounded by protective white light and positive energy. As I prepare to leave my body to experience other realities, I am fully infused with peace and serenity. Throughout this experience, I will be shielded from all harm—mentally, physically, and spiritually— by the guiding powers of higher astral planes. My physical body at rest will remain safely enveloped in positive energy as I journey to other realities. I will return safely to my body at any moment by simply deciding to do so. Upon my return, my total being will be refreshed, invigorated, and empowered.*

Following these affirmations, imagining consciousness as a white light rising gently from the body is often introduced, a process aided by images of motion. Floating balloons, or a white sail pushed gently by a breeze, are good images to focus on. Following a few moments in which the mental pictures become progressively clearer, the physical body, safely enfolded in a protective glow, is usually envisioned from overhead until full awareness of being out-of-body occurs. The out-of-body state typically emerges gradually as sensations of weightlessness and floating gently upward. Occasionally, however, the out-of-body state will occur instantly as a forceful separation of the astral from the physical body.

Step 2: Travel

Intent to consciously experience a location distant from the physical body typically initiates out-of-body flight. The destination can be either designated or open-ended. It can be a tangible site or an intangible dimension. Once a sense of separation from the body is fully established, mental images of the destination and, whenever possible, the route to be taken to it, can aid travel. For distant tangible locations, images of a map or globe with destinations highlighted, followed by aerial images of the destination, can be very effective. For intangible destinations, such as a higher astral plane, images of a dimension filled with light are often useful. For spontaneous flights, travel unfolds independently of direct guidance. Like out-of-body induction, travel to distant destinations can occur either gradually or instantly. Many experienced travelers report that once out-of-body, they can automatically be wherever they choose to be at the moment.

Step 3: Destination

A wide range of empowering activities, including observations, interactions, and goal-related activities, can unfold upon arrival at the destination. This is the empowering peak of most OBEs. At this point, critical insight and highly significant knowledge often emerge. Astral interactions initiated at this stage can be profoundly empowering.

Step 4: Return

Although a variety of OBEs return strategies have been developed, the typical return procedure is usually initiated simply by a deliberate intent to re-engage the physical body. As in astral travel to a distant location, the return destination is envisioned—in this case, the physical body at rest—followed by travel itself. Once in the presence of the physical body, the astral body is mentally guided to gently re-engage with the physical body. Although the return and re-entry is usually gradual, many experienced travelers report the ability to reunite almost instantly with the physical body. Following re-entry, attention is usually focused on breathing and various other physical sensations. A brief concluding period of reflection and resolution maximizes the empowering benefits of the experience.

Although we can occasionally encounter negative conditions during OBEs, the out-of-body state does not automatically increase our vulnerability to negative energies. We are, in fact, *better* equipped in the out-of-body state than in the typical biologically engaged state to counteract negative force fields and opposing influences. In the out-of-body state, the astral body is liberated from biological constraints, and once enveloped in its own positive force field and shielded with positive astral energies, it can effectively discern and repel any negative field it encounters. Positive astral energy will consistently counteract the threat of all opposing energy forces. Infused with positive astral energy, we are fully able to dissolve the pockets of negative energy that could hamper astral travel or in other ways thwart the astral experience. Because they exercise our coping and defense capacities, OBEs as growth strategies increase our power to overcome the negative forces we all encounter in daily life.

Over recent years, several highly effective step-by-step OBEs strategies have been developed in our laboratories. Some of these strategies are based on analyses of procedures used by experienced subjects outside the laboratory; the others originated in the laboratory. All, however, were tested for effectiveness under stringently controlled conditions. While some of the procedures were designed for highly specific empowerment purposes, others were developed simply as general practice exercises for building the out-of-body skills required for a wide range of empowerment goals.

Several of the strategies developed in our laboratories were found to have important practice value as well as multiple applications. Among the most highly effective of these strategies are *OBEs Levitation, Astral Walk, Mirror Image,* and *Astral Surfing.* Interestingly, gender differences in the effectiveness of these procedures have been noted, with women typically more responsive to Mirror Image and men typically more responsive to Astral Walk. OBEs Levitation and Astral Surfing were found to be equally effective for men and women. These four procedures, as detailed in the following discussion, are flexible and can be altered as needed to meet individual preferences and styles. They can be easily revised to fit individual comfort zones and to incorporate a wide range of empowering resources, such as ministering angels and spirit guides. Each procedure emphasizes personal responsibility, motivation, and clearly formulated goals as the primary components shaping the empowerment outcome. Approximately one hour, during which there are no distractions, should be set aside for each procedure.

OBEs Levitation

OBEs Levitation is an interactive induction procedure that uses impressions of physical weightlessness to facilitate astral disengagement from the physical body. Spontaneous OBEs are often initiated by sensations of slowly drifting upward and away from the physical body as it remains at rest. OBEs Levitation promotes that natural out-of-body phenomenon by deliberately introducing physical sensations of weightlessness, followed by imagery of the biological body levitating and then returning to its original position, but with the astral body remaining in the levitated state.

OBEs Levitation requires only sensations of biological levitation, not actual levitation. The rationale for this procedure is that sensations of biological levitation can literally release the astral body from the physical body, thereby producing astral levitation. Here is the eight-step procedure:

Step 1. While in a comfortable, reclining position, mentally scan your total body, pausing at areas of tension and letting them relax. Slow your breathing, taking a little longer to exhale, until you develop a relaxed, effortless breathing pattern.

Step 2. Focus your full attention on your physical body and imagine it becoming lighter and lighter, until finally, it seems to become weightless.

Step 3. As the sense of weightlessness continues, imagine your physical body, as light as a feather, beginning to rise slowly. Next, envision your physical body momentarily suspended in space, then slowly returning to its original position, but leaving your consciousness behind in astral form, still suspended over your physical body.

Step 4. From overhead, view your physical body, now resting comfortably below. Notice your sense of weightlessness and separation from your physical body.

Step 5. Invoke the positive energies of higher astral planes by envisioning your projected astral body, as well as your physical body below, surrounded by white radiance, then affirming:

My total being is now enveloped in the powerful radiance of cosmic energy. As I travel, I will be empowered and protected, mentally, physically, and spiritually, by the positive energies of higher astral planes. I will return to my physical body at any time by simple intent alone.

Step 6. Give yourself permission to travel to any pre-determined destination, or simply allow travel to unfold effortlessly and spontaneously. Make in-flight corrections, as needed, by consciously intervening into the out-of-body experience. Reaffirm periodically the presence of powerful cosmic energy infusing your total being, including your physical body as it rests safely at a distance.

Step 7. To return to your physical body, envision it in its familiar setting, then simply affirm your intent to return to it. Once in the presence of your physical body, passively at rest, give yourself permission to re-unite with it. Upon re-engaging your body, notice your breathing and various other physical sensations.

Step 8. Conclude the procedure with a brief period of rest and reflection. Give particular attention to the empowerment benefits of the experience.

OBEs Levitation is valued not only as an effective practice procedure for developing out-of-body skills, it has also gained recognition as an important health and fitness tool. Individuals who routinely practice this procedure invariably experience a general improvement in their mental and physical health. They become less anxious and more energetic. They develop a more optimistic outlook and a more positive self-image. The procedure has been highly effective in weight management and stop-smoking programs when combined with pre- and post-induction conditioning that included affirmations designed to build self-esteem and a success orientation.

Astral Walk

While walking is usually considered simply a physical activity, it can be seen metaphorically as a social, psychological, and psychical phenomenon. In our interpersonal relations, for instance, we adjust social distance by mentally walking toward, away from, and with people. *Astral Walk* is an OBEs procedure that introduces out-of-body walking as a figurative phenomenon: Astrally, we walk away from the physical body and into the astral travel mode. At the end of out-of-body travel, we walk back into the body.

Astral Walk is a structured, seven-step procedure designed to generate an empowered mental state and productive out-of-body travel. The procedure identifies the three essential components of empowering OBEs as peace, balance, and harmony, and assigns each component a color. The three colors are then blended to give substance to the astral body which is then readily envisioned. The blending process is not required to follow the principles of color mixing, and can produce any shade of any color, as well as pure white. The colors black or gray, however, are not recommended as astral colors, because of the potentially disempowering frequencies of these colors when assigned to the astral body. Here is the procedure:

Step 1. Inner Peace. Assume a relaxed position, and develop a slow, rhythmic breathing pattern. It may help to breathe deeply and slowly for a few moments while focusing only on your breathing. Mentally scan your physical body, pausing at points of tension and allowing relaxation to soak deep into the muscles and joints of your body.

Once your body is fully relaxed, clear your mind by letting go of all active thought. Imagine your thoughts as having wings, taking off and disappearing into the distance until all that remains behind is peace of mind. Picture peace of mind as a soft pastel color, then affirm: *I am at complete peace.*

Step 2. Inner Balance. With your body relaxed and your mind at peace, picture the innermost core of your being actively radiating harmony and balancing you mentally, physically, and spiritually. As you sense that balanced vibration, assign it a vibrant color that infuses your total being.

Step 3. Cosmic Harmony. Picture the vast universe and let yourself become an integral part of it. Envision the starry heavens and the distant reaches of space. Imagine other distant dimensions, and planes far beyond the reach of our most powerful telescopes. As you reflect on the limitlessness of the universe, notice your sense of cosmic harmony, and assign it a color. Allow that color to surround you and totally permeate your being. Affirm: *I am a part of all that exists.*

Step 4. Astral Power. Envision the three colors representing peace, balance, and cosmic harmony merging, coming together, to form a fourth color signifying cosmic power. Envision your astral body soaking in the coloration of cosmic power.

Step 5. Astral Walk-out. This critical step introduces the out-of-body experience. As your biological body remains at rest, invoke the protection of higher astral planes and affirm: *I am now ready to leave my body. My total being—mental, physical, and spiritual—will be protected and secure as I travel out-of-body.*

Take in a few very deep breaths, and upon slowly exhaling, sense the pleasant disengagement and projection of your astral body, smoothly rising above your biological body and taking on the coloration of cosmic power as designated in Step 4 above. Notice your sense of freedom and release. You are now prepared to travel out-of-body into realities beyond your present environment.

Step 6: Astral Travel. To step into the astral travel mode, affirm: *I am now empowered to travel wherever I wish to go. Intent alone is sufficient to take me to distant destinations and bring me back to my physical body. As I travel, I will be enveloped in protective energy. My physical body at rest will be safe, secure, and fully infused with positive energy.*

Envision your astral destination and give yourself permission to travel to it. Focus on the destination until you sense its presence. Upon reaching your destination, you can initiate relevant out-of-body activities at will.

Step 7. The Return. You can end out-of-body travel and reunite with your physical body at any point during the experience by simply affirming your intent to return and envisioning your physical body at rest in its familiar setting. Given these conditions, the re-engagement process is usually smooth and effortless.

Step 8. Resolution. Upon reuniting with your physical body, again envision the three colors representing peace, balance, and cosmic harmony coming together to form the color of cosmic power. Sense the quiet blending of colors and the ensuing infusion of power. Conclude the experience by affirming: *I am now infused with abundant cosmic power. I am at complete peace and total harmony with the universe.*

Mirror Image

Although the mirror is often viewed as a somewhat less than elegant tool for out-of-body induction, its usefulness has been repeatedly demonstrated both in the laboratory setting and in OBEs training programs. As an OBEs tool, the mirror provides an external point of focus that facilitates imagery and concentration, both of which help exteriorize awareness and produce the out-of-body state. The mirror is also useful as an OBEs resolution tool because of its capacity to give empowering substance to post-OBEs affirmations.

Mirror Image requires either a wall-mounted or free-standing full-length mirror for out-of-body induction in an upright, seated position.

For induction in the reclining or lying position, an overhead full-length mirror is required. Here is the procedure:

Step 1. Formulate your OBEs objectives. Your objective may be simply to explore Mirror Image as an induction procedure, or you may wish to travel out-of-body to a specified destination to achieve a particular empowerment goal.

Step 2. Having formulated your objectives, settle back and, as you become relaxed, view yourself in the mirror, paying particular attention to your eyes. Think of them as "windows of the soul."

Step 3. While focusing on your eyes, expand your peripheral vision to take in your total body. Then further expand your visual field to take in the full mirror and its surroundings. Expand your peripheral vision to its limits, and let your eyes fall slightly out of focus. You will then notice the so-called "white-out effect" in which your visual field takes on a whitish glow. At that point, notice the relaxation deepening as you become increasingly tranquil and serene.

Step 4. Return your focus to your eyes, and again think of them as windows of the soul.

Step 5. After a few moments of focusing your full attention on your eyes, imagine your image in the mirror as your true self. Then, shift your awareness onto that image by imagining yourself on the other side of the mirror. From your position beyond the mirror, view your physical body, paying particular attention again to your eyes. Sense the distance between yourself and your physical body. Should your awareness begin to slip back to your physical body, shift it back to your image beyond the mirror. With practice, this process becomes increasingly easy.

Step 6. Once your awareness is comfortably settled into the image of yourself beyond the mirror, close your eyes and picture your physical body resting at a distance, enveloped in the bright radiance of cosmic energy.

Step 7. Envision your astral being surrounded by the glow of powerful white energy, and invoke the protection of higher astral planes. Affirm: *I am fully infused—mentally, physically, and spiritually—with radiant energy. I am secure and fully protected. I can re-engage my physical body at will.*

Step 8. At this step, direct the out-of-body experience toward your previously stated goals. You may wish simply to experience the out-of-body state, or you may prefer to travel to a particular destination. You may wish to access and interact with distant physical realities or higher astral planes. You can also initiate spontaneous or exploratory travel at this level.

Step 9. To end out-of-body travel, envision your physical body resting passively in its familiar surroundings while giving yourself permission to re-engage it. Continue to envision your physical body until you sense its presence and a full sense of being re-united with it emerges.

Step 10. Conclude the procedure by first noticing the various sensations of your physical body, and then, upon opening your eyes and viewing yourself in the mirror, affirming: *As I view myself in the mirror, I see my true self—secure, self-confident, and totally empowered.*

Astral Surfing

Astral Surfing is an advanced out-of-body method using highly flexible induction and management procedures. It emphasizes spontaneous out-of-body exploration of the cosmos in the absence of structured limits or specifically defined goals. The scope of surfing is expansive and comprises a sweeping survey of many astral options. Surfing the cosmos can be compared to surfing the lyceum hall with its inspirational lectures, concerts, and entertainments. It is based on the premise that consciousness in the out-of-body state can scan the universe, surf among rich astral planes, and discover new realms of pleasure and power. Astral Surfing is a valued strategy for unleashing hidden intellectual and creative potentials. Not surprisingly, peak insights and optimal solutions often emanate from Astral Surfing.

Astral Surfing requires conditions similar to other OBEs induction and management procedures—a firm resolve to experience the out-of-body state, appropriate safeguards, and empowering imagery and affirmations. This strategy differs, however, from other methods, in that it provides a highly pliable framework for exploring the universe and surfing among astral planes. Astral Surfing suggests options rather than prescribing procedures. This flexible approach recognizes individual differences in the ability to independently direct the astral experience while in the out-of-body state. Here is the five-step procedure:

Step 1. Preliminary Considerations. A period of at least one hour, during which brief, periodic re-engagements of the physical body can occur, is recommended for surfing. These transient re-entries provide brief rest periods within a series of flights while enhancing the effectiveness of surfing and preventing post-flight fatigue. Invocations that assure complete cosmic protection through affirmations and imagery of being encased in light are recommended at the beginning and periodically throughout the procedure.

Step 2. Induction. To induce the out-of-body state, settle back and let your physical body become progressively relaxed as your thoughts become increasingly passive. Envisioning an astral flight vehicle—such as a crystalline capsule or carpet of energy—bearing consciousness in astral body form upward and away from your physical body can facilitate induction of the out-of-body state. Imagery of the flight vehicle is likewise effective for periodic re-entries and re-induction following rest intervals.

Step 3. Surfing. To initiate surfing, envision the three-dimensional *cosmic design* of the universe with flight pathways among cosmic points, dimensions, and planes. *Points* in the cosmic design signify brilliant concentrations of cosmic energy, with the colors of a given point denoting its particular power capacities, for example, green signifies healing, yellow signifies intellectual power, and blue signifies serenity. Cosmic points can be aligned along an inviting surfing thoroughfare, or they can exist as isolated concentrations of bright, interacting energies.

In contrast to points, *cosmic dimensions* are large domains of energy in the cosmic design, glowing and radiating power. Dimensions vary in size, color, intensity, and shape. Some are so distant that they are barely visible to the astral eye, whereas others dominate the cosmic structure. Certain expansive dimensions embody constellations of bright cosmic points and planes, whereas others emit only a soft, inviting cosmic glow.

Cosmic planes are represented by layers of radiant energy in the cosmic design, with each layer differing in design and color. Certain planes appear rugged and irregular, whereas others are smooth and elegant. Some planes exist as components of complex astral dimensions, while others appear apart from other cosmic elements. Like certain cosmic dimensions, some planes seem almost impenetrable, while others challenge contact and interaction.

Surfing among points, dimensions, and planes can be either spontaneous or destination-oriented. Spontaneous surfing occurs effortlessly and requires no astral itinerary or flight plan. You can glide freely in and out of planes and dimensions, stopping over at will, then sliding forward to other destinations. You can interface with cosmic points to draw energy from them, or slip into dimensions and planes to access their empowering properties whenever needed. In contrast to spontaneous surfing, destination-oriented surfing requires deliberately choosing particular pathways as travel routes to designated dimensions, points, or planes.

Step 4. Astral Return. To end out-of-body travel, simply envision your physical body in its familiar setting and affirm your intent to return to it. A sense of presence in the body accompanied by specific physical sensations signals a successful re-entry. This procedure is effective for transient re-entries during Astral Surfing as well as the concluding astral return.

Step 5. Conclusion. Conclude Astral surfing by briefly reviewing the experience and reflecting on its empowering effects.

In summary, the strategies presented in this chapter are designed to build basic out-of-body induction and management skills. They prepare us for the more advanced procedures designed to meet highly specific empowerment needs, such as health and fitness, the development of our psychic abilities, discarnate interactions, and past-life enlightenment. In the chapters that follow, we will explore many specialized out-of-body strategies and their applications, with special emphasis on the empowering potential and practical value of each strategy.

4

OBEs and ESP

Knowledge is the true origin of sight, not the eyes.

Panchatantra

THE UNIVERSE, BY its existence alone, commands our attention, exploration, and interaction. We are, by our nature as human beings, endowed with the capacity to explore, discover, and interact with our environment, from our most immediate surroundings to the farthest reaches of space. But we have, as previously noted, scarcely begun to develop that potential. Even our deepest probes of the physical universe have, at best, barely scratched the surface. Although a massive body of constantly evolving knowledge is now at our command, we remain but a minnow in a small village stream—isolated and confined within the narrow limits of our existence.

The constricted range of our awareness applies not only to the outer universe, but to our inner selves as well. We have, for instance, only recently recognized the empowering potential of the complex interactions between the mind and body, including the capacity of the mind to alter body chemistry, control pain, accelerate healing, promote wellness, slow aging, and even repair damaged neural connections in the brain, to list a few of the amazing possibilities. Notwithstanding our many recent advances, the observations of Pascal in 1670 continue to explain the current state of our progress:

> Man is to himself the most wonderful object in nature; for he cannot conceive what the body is, still less what the mind is, and least of all how a body should be united with a mind.

The mind-body connection, while continuing to command our attention, remains largely an unsolved mystery.

The psychic nature of our being is possibly the last great frontier in our search for knowledge and understanding. Today, as never before, we are challenged not only to explore that frontier and make some sense of it, but to develop a new psychic technology that benefits everyone, both now and in the future. The starting point must be a raised psychic consciousness and a firm commitment to explore and actualize our highest potentials, including our extrasensory capacities.

Extrasensory perception (ESP) is usually defined as the knowledge of, or response to, external events or situations independent of sensory mechanisms or processes. Together, *physical sensation* and *sensory perception* link the brain to the world around us. Physical sensation is the immediate and direct result of stimulating our many physical senses, including seeing, hearing, touching, smelling, and tasting. Sensory perception is our interpretation of sensory stimulation. ESP, on the other hand, requires no physical stimulation of our sensory mechanisms. Our extrasensory channels are typically sharpened by a quiet mental state and a reduction in sensory stimulation. Although ESP can use many tangible objects to induce a psychically responsive state or to stimulate extrasensory channels, our perceptions are extrasensory only to the degree that they do not depend on sensory experience. *As adaptive creatures, we need not only sensory-based awareness of the world around us, we also need expanded knowledge of other realities not available through sensory experience alone.* Our higher evolution is, consequently, inextricably linked to our psychic unfolding.

Our ESP potential includes expanded psychic awareness of the past (*retrocognition*), present (*clairvoyance*), and future (*precognition*), as well as the perception of another person's thoughts or psychological state (*telepathy*). Although these abilities exist in everyone to some degree, none of us has fully developed them. Actualizing our inner potential, whether psychic, scientific, artistic, musical, linguistic, athletic, or any other, requires practice and experience. Even the most talented psychic luminaries, like gifted celebrities in other fields, find that practice and experience, along with commitment and hard work, are critical to the mastery of their craft. Unfortunately, the development of our psychic skills has been left largely to chance or trial and error. Although some psychic unfolding will probably occur spontaneously in everyone, the full realization of our multiple psychic abilities requires concentrated effort within a plan that is both comprehensive and specialized.

The out-of-body experience is a critical component in any psychic development plan because it puts our psychic capacities *online* and readies them for action and growth. Our laboratory studies revealed that OBEs almost invariably stimulate some form of extrasensory expression. Because consciousness is separated from physiology during the out-of-body state, OBEs are not only extra-biological, but also extra-sensory. Such a concept must, however, allow for individual differences in perception and for a margin of error, even in the out-of-body state, during which we continue to experience and interpret reality from our own frame of reference. The out-of-body state does not produce robot-like people with perceptual conformity—we remain individuals with our unique tendencies, preferences, inclinations, and predispositions. Along with our strengths and virtues, our weaknesses and imperfections endure, uninterrupted by the out-of-body state. It should not be surprising then to find that individual differences in perceptual accuracy also survive in the real-life world of OBEs.

A study conducted in our laboratory to investigate ESP during the out-of-body state found significant improvements in telepathy, precognition, and clairvoyance when compared to previous ESP performance. On average, the accuracy of all forms of ESP improved by around 50 percent during the out-of-body state. Clairvoyance improved by the greatest margin—approximately 75 percent. This dramatic increase could be explained as out-of-body travel rather than clairvoyance, since the experimental task required describing in detail an art object located in a distant setting. Telepathy, requiring the sending and receiving of critical elements in a paragraph, improved by more than 45 percent. For this task, the sender, prior to out-of-body induction, was given the contents of the paragraph and instructed to later send them to the target receiver while both were in the out-of-body state. An improvement of around 25 percent was found for precognition, which required subjects to predict the next-day stock-market performance of the NYSE. Given the nature of the out-of-body state and the liberation of psychic faculties that accompany it, an increase in psychic performance during that state would seem a reasonable expectation.

Following the introduction of OBEs into our experimental psychic development program, more and more of our subjects reported occasionally entering an astral dimension and literally being instructed by astral guides on how to develop their psychic potential. An interesting consistency was noted from subject to subject in the concepts and strategies presented to them by their various astral guides. Invariably, practice and meditation were stressed as critical to psychic growth. Also, creative activities designed to develop imagery powers and expand cognitive functions were strongly emphasized. Occasionally, the astral guides recommended highly specific strategies, including empowering affirmations and simple physical gestures, such as joining the tips of the fingers to activate precognition and touching the forehead to activate clairvoyance. To activate telepathy, the guides often recommended some form of imagery, such as using imaginary symbols to condense thoughts, or mentally erecting a communication channel of light between the sender and receiver.

Based on the result of our laboratory studies, along with the analysis of many reports of ESP-related OBEs outside the laboratory, we developed different ESP strategies for telepathy, clairvoyance, and pre-cognition, with the out-of-body state as the centerpiece for each strategy. Each strategy is unique in both the induction method used to produce the out-of-body state and the management procedures applied to direct the out-of-body experience. Outweighing these exclusive features, however, are certain common elements, the most important of these being the superior role of consciousness in the out-of-body state to voluntarily call forth and unleash our psychic powers. A second common element is the fundamental goal of the strategies: the full development of our psychic abilities as tools for growth and discovery.

Out-of-Body Telepathy

Telepathy is usually considered the most common type of extrasensory perception. Because it often occurs effortlessly and subconsciously, it may also be the most common form of human interaction. Telepathy is, in fact, often seen as a spontaneous, on-going phenomenon in everyone. Moreover, there is considerable evidence to suggest that telepathy is common among animals, including the capacity to communicate psychically with people. Strong human and animal bonds are often characterized by very meaningful telepathic interactions. Many highly advanced telepathic expressions are seen in the behaviors of the so-called "lower animals."

Similar to other communication models, telepathy requires three essential components: a sender, a receiver, and a communication channel. Occurring either spontaneously or voluntarily, telepathy is one of the most powerful communication tools known. Telepathy can reach far beyond the simple communication of thought contents. It can generate complex telepathic interactions that induce positive changes in mental functions and mood states. It can expand our psychic as well as non-psychic communication channels and enrich our interactions with others. It can be directed inwardly as positive thoughts to empower oneself, or it can be directed outwardly to empower others. It can build self-esteem, generate peace of mind, promote well-being, and unleash abundant new growth possibilities in oneself and others alike.

More importantly, while positively motivated telepathy is empowering to sender and receiver alike, negatively motivated telepathy is selectively disempowering to the sender alone. Psychic messages designed to disempower others automatically block the communication channel and "bounce back" to disempower the sender.

Telepathy can occur at both individual and group levels. While telepathy at the individual level can be mutually empowering to both sender and receiver, telepathic energies generated by groups can go forth in sufficient power to influence not only individual and group behavior, but global conditions as well. Conceivably, messages of peace generated on a massive scale could raise global consciousness and literally generate world peace. Similarly, messages of love could make the planet more compassionate, and motivate us, individually and collectively, to solve problems such as hunger, disease, and injustice, wherever they are found on the planet.

In the group setting, we often observe *empathic telepathy,* in which the individual receiver inadvertently sends the communication to other group members. Empathic telepathy illustrates the potential control problems inherent in laboratory studies of ESP. Even persons outside the laboratory can be the recipients and senders of telepathic messages generated in the laboratory setting. While this phenomenon presents a serious control challenge in the experimental setting, it suggests almost unlimited possibilities for the global application of telepathy. Positive telepathic messages sent forth into the universe will indeed find a receiving audience.

Our laboratory studies of out-of-body telepathy were designed to explore new options for developing out telepathic faculties and using them to bring forth positive change. The studies typically involved person-to-person telepathy in which either the sender or the receiver, and in some instances both, were in the out-of-body state. Almost without exception, improved performance in both sending and receiving was noted during the out-of-body state. Perhaps as expected, the best results were obtained when both the sender and the receiver were in the out-of-body state.

Although shorter distances between sender and receiver appear to improve performance in non-OBEs telepathy, spatial distance becomes less relevant when either sender or receiver is in the out-of-body state. On average, out-of-body telepathy in the laboratory is as effective for individuals in close proximity as when separated by several hundred miles. This suggests an astral dimension in which our conventional concepts of physical space and distance simply do not apply. It further suggests the clear advantage of out-of-body telepathy over conventional telepathy when used on a global scale.

As already noted, the presence of astral guides, who are constantly poised to promote our growth, is particularly evident in the out-of-body state. Many of our research subjects reported out-of-body interactions with highly advanced *communication guides,* who assisted them in sending and receiving telepathic messages. One subject reported an out-of-body interaction with his communication guide in which he received highly specific instructions on how to communicate telepathically. According to his guide, we communicate in many ways, and we can master them all. His guide advised that by focusing on the inner region of the forehead of oneself and another, we can establish a psychic communication link with that person for sending and receiving telepathic messages. According to his guide, the technique is equally effective when the receiving subject is not present. Astral guides consistently emphasized the ethical responsibility of using our psychic skills in positive ways that promote the well-being of ourselves and others. This is the cardinal principle underlying all psychic development, according to astral communication guides. Self-interest alone is insufficient motivation for developing and using our telepathic powers.

Although we may make no concentrated effort during OBEs to communicate telepathically, the telepathic potential is clearly amplified and placed in a state of readiness. Telepathy during OBEs seems to have its own guidance system, which can seek out the target receiver and deliver its empowering payload. That spontaneous capacity is supplemented by deliberately formulating the telepathic message and mentally releasing it. The critical force energizing the total system is the out-of-body state.

The Astral Telepathy System

The *Astral Telepathy System* (ATS) is an OBEs induction and telepathic sending system that utilizes imagery during the out-of-body state to bring the psychic message into clear focus, and deliver it to the target receiver. As an interactive, consciousness-to-consciousness system, ATS requires no out-of-body travel over spatial distance to locate the telepathic receiver. Even when the physical location of the receiver is unknown, imagery of the receiver is usually sufficient to activate the message and project it to its targeted destination—the consciousness of the receiver.

Central to ATS is the *Astral Blue Beltway*, a fluid stream of psychic energy used to convey telepathic messages. We have known for years that blue imagery is one of the most effective tools known for activating telepathic sending. In the controlled laboratory setting, senders and receivers who envisioned blue, such as a pale blue moon on which the psychic message appeared, or a blue sky against which clouds formed the psychic communication, consistently performed at a superior level. Imagery of blue may have literally accessed the Astral Blue Beltway that, in turn, channeled the message to the designated receiver. When introduced during the out-of-body state, blue imagery, such as a blue mist enveloping the astral body, effectively engages the Astral Blue Beltway as a dynamic communication system with unprecedented accuracy. ATS consists of nine essential steps. Here is the procedure:

Step 1. Before entering the out-of-body state, formulate your telepathic message in ways that use both language and symbols. Symbols are important in telepathy, because they condense telepathic communications into a form easily envisioned and projected to the target receiver. Familiar symbols are particularly effective. For instance, imagery of a dove can be used to transport a message of peace. Similarly, imagery of a heart superimposed with the word *love* can be used to communicate the message, *I love you*. Imagery of colorful balloons with words such as *happiness, blessings*, and *congratulations* are likewise effective. Although symbols are highly useful in opening psychic channels and conveying simple messages in condensed form, complex psychic sending and receiving interactions usually require more advanced procedures with the capacity to amplify and personalize messages beyond the limited meanings of a single word or a selected symbol.

Step 2. Having formulated your ATS objectives, find a comfortable, quiet place and allow yourself about thirty minutes for the session. Loosen any tight-fitting clothing and lie down on a bed or couch. Slow your breathing and scan your body from your forehead to your feet, releasing all tension until your body is fully relaxed. Tell yourself, *Time is slowing down. I have plenty of time to relax.*

Step 3. With your body now completely relaxed, affirm, *I am protected and secure as I prepare to leave my body*. Envision your body at rest, surrounded by a glowing aura of empowering cosmic energy. Continue to envision your biological body at rest until you become aware of your presence outside your body. This is typically a gradual process that requires only a few moments.

Step 4. Once you are aware of the out-of-body state, view your physical body at rest, enveloped in the protective glow of cosmic energy. Then mentally envelop your astral body in radiant blue light and affirm:

> *I am surrounded by the positive energies of the universe. My innermost being and the highest powers of the cosmos are now poised to merge in a powerful interaction. I am now at my peak of psychic empowerment. As I remain out-of-body, my telepathic faculties are fully liberated. I am empowered to end the out-of-body state and freely re-engage my physical body at any moment through mere intent alone.*

Step 5. As you continue the out-of-body state, review your previously formulated telepathic message, giving particular attention to both language and symbols.

Step 6. Focus your attention on your telepathic receiver, and momentarily, you will notice the Astral Blue Beltway, a soft blue stream of energy connecting you to your target. Release your telepathic thoughts and images, and let them flow freely on the blue beltway. Envision them as they travel the beltway. Allow adequate time for the psychic messages to reach their designated target, keeping your psychic sending and receiving channels open until the psychic process runs its course.

Step 7. Close down the process by turning your attention to your biological body at rest, then giving yourself permission to re-engage it.

Step 8. Upon re-engagement, briefly note any physical sensations, such the position or weight of your body.

Step 9. Conclude the procedure with a quiet period of reflection, followed by the simple affirmation: *I am empowered and fully infused with the highest energies of the universe.*

Out-of-Body Clairvoyance

Clairvoyance, like telepathy and precognition, often occurs spontaneously during the out-of-body state. With the physical body in a passive, restful state, consciousness is liberated to more fully experience itself and exercise its highest faculties, among them its clairvoyant powers. Strategies that utilize the out-of-body state are among the best procedures known for exercising and developing our clairvoyant powers.

Clairvoyance is usually defined as the extrasensory perception of objects, conditions, situations, and events. It can include psychic awareness of current happenings, the location of lost items, the mental state of an individual, or the situational factors influencing one's behaviors. In its most advanced form, clairvoyance includes not only specific impressions, but a comprehensive, panoramic view of all relevant variables, a phenomenon we call *astral scan*. Motivational factors and a vast range of emotional variables are all within the scope of astral scan. This scanning feature of clairvoyance is critical to a variety of psychic applications, including criminal investigation, managerial and organizational consultation, and personal counseling.

Astral Sweep

Since spontaneous but usually unfocused psychic scanning often occurs during the out-of-body state, a procedure called *Astral Sweep* was developed to deliberately evoke out-of-body clairvoyant scanning, in either open-ended or focused form. In its open-ended form, astral sweep surveys conditions, events, or situations independently of specific limits, whereas in its focused form, the sweep is directed to designated targets. Both forms are similar in that no restrictions are placed on the extent of the clairvoyant sweep in uncovering relevant information. Both forms view clairvoyant insight as purposeful and potentially empowering.

This out-of-body procedure does not require, but can include, astral travel to distant destinations. Here is the seven-step procedure:

Step 1. Statement of Goals. For the focused form of the procedure, formulate your goals around a particular target situation or condition. You may, for instance, focus on a particular individual, a specific geographical setting, a certain event, or a given situation. For the open-ended form of the procedure, formulate your goals in general terms, thus allowing your clairvoyant faculty to select its own target situation and access any information related to it.

Step 2. Out-of-Body Induction. For this procedure, the recommended out-of-body induction strategy is called upward scan. While in a relaxed, reclining position, envision yourself surrounded and protected by the glow of empowering cosmic energy. Picture relaxation as a fog spreading slowly over your physical body from your feet upward until your body is fully enveloped. Envision the fog then slowly lifting from your body, with your consciousness rising gently with it. Once your consciousness is suspended, view your body resting comfortably below. Affirm:

> *I am fully empowered and protected mentally, physically, and spiritually by the highest powers of the cosmos. I can return to my body at will by simply deciding to do so.*

Step 3. Activating Out-of-Body Clairvoyance. Once the out-of-body state has been achieved, the metaphor of mountain climbing is introduced to activate clairvoyance. Envision yourself as a psychic explorer, slowly ascending an astral mountain from its base to its peak. Each step upward expands the scope of your clairvoyant powers. Allow yourself plenty of time to scale the mountain and experience the progressive release of your psychic potentials. When you finally reach the summit, your psychic scanning powers are at their peak.

Step 4. Clairvoyant Sweeping. As already noted, clairvoyant sweeping can be either open-ended or focused. For open-ended sweeping, survey the surrounding reality from your astral observation point at the mountain's peak. With your clairvoyant powers now fully activated and free of constrictions, you can probe the most distant realities and access the highest sources of knowledge. Allow your clairvoyant powers to gather relevant information from any source, zooming in for a closer look whenever necessary. For focused clairvoyant sweeping, center your scanning efforts on certain designated targets, and scan their surroundings for additional information as desired. Continue scanning until you gather the information you need.

Step 5. Astral Travel (Optional). Astral travel to distant destinations during scanning can be useful in gathering additional, highly detailed information, or in accessing higher astral planes. Travel can be initiated following either open-ended or focused sweeping by first centering your attention on the desired destination and then intentionally engaging it as a present reality. In the out-of-body state, intent alone is usually sufficient to engage even the most distant reality.

Step 6. The Return. Reuniting with your physical body is initiated by the simple intent to reunite with your body, envisioning your body in its familiar surroundings, and giving yourself permission to re-engage it. The simple affirmation, *I will now re-unite with my body*, facilitates an easy re-entry. The return is concluded by focusing on various physical sensations and affirming, *I am now at oneness with my body and the universe*.

Step 7. Resolution and Reflection. Review the out-of-body experience, paying particular attention to the clairvoyant information derived from it. Reflecting on the experience, if only briefly, dramatically increases its empowering effects.

Although Astral Sweep can be used to survey cosmic planes and initiate empowering interactions with them, it has many highly practical, down-to-earth applications. It is particularly useful in locating lost animals and personal items. A student trained in Astral Sweep decided to use the technique to locate a horse that had wandered into the countryside. Through astrally surveying the surrounding wilderness, he located the horse grazing peacefully with other horses in a remote wasteland. Another student, also trained in astral sweep, used the technique to recover a lost bracelet. Through astral sweep, she discovered the bracelet near a park bench where she had joined a friend for lunch the previous day.

Astral Sweep is also useful as a criminal investigative procedure for surveying crime scenes and gathering relevant information. In one case, a psychic consultant used the procedure to locate a kidnap victim being held for ransom. Using a combination of open-ended sweeping and focusing, the psychic located the mountain cabin where the victim was being held, and then zoomed in to gather critical information that led to a successful rescue.

Although clairvoyant scanning can occur using other less-specialized OBEs procedures, Astral Sweep is often preferred because of its functional design and high degree of accuracy. Given even moderate practice, almost everyone will discover the practical benefits of this useful procedure.

Out-of-Body Precognition

Precognition, or psychic perception of the future, empowers each of us to reach beyond the present and embrace the future with increased awareness and confidence. To disregard our precognitive powers is like sitting on a treasure chest filled with immeasurable wealth and never opening the chest. Precognition reveals the wondrous opportunities that await us and prepares us to make the best of them. It forewarns and allows us to prevent, avoid, or prepare for formidable events. It helps decision-making by predicting consequences and suggesting optimal courses of action. On a global scale, precognition challenges us to avoid sweeping crises and bring into existence a civilization committed to peace and progress.

From the psychic empowerment perspective, psychic predictions are usually seen not as absolute certainties, but rather as forecasts with varying degrees of probability. But determining the probability level of a prediction, whether psychic or otherwise, is not always easy. Future outcomes can almost always be influenced by intervening variables, some of which may be beyond our control, but the most important of which are often our own actions. Precognition can arm us with new information, more options, better choices, and greater mastery of the forces that influence our lives.

The out-of-body state often activates our precognitive powers and centers them on what we need to know at the moment. In fact, the primary focus of many spontaneous OBEs seems to be on precognitive awareness. This is perhaps due to the capacity of the out-of-body state to put us *on line with the future* by either accessing the inner sources of precognition or tapping into outer realms of precognitive knowledge.

Two laboratory-tested strategies have been designed specifically to activate out-of-body precognition. The first, *Personal Exposé*, is a self-contained approach that focuses on the internal sources of precognitive awareness. Its objectives, are first, to uncover precognitive knowledge already existing within the subconscious mind, and second, to activate the inner precognitive mechanisms required to generate totally new precognitive knowledge.

The second approach, *Cosmic Exposé*, is other-world oriented. It focuses on precognitive sources beyond the self and the realm of material reality. Cosmic Exposé typically involves out-of-body travel to distant dimensions and interactions with higher cosmic sources of knowledge.

Both Personal and Cosmic Exposé require a physical setting somewhat different from other procedures, with an expansive, open environment preferred. In our OBEs studies, the precognitive performance of both Personal and Cosmic Exposé subjects dramatically improved when they went from the laboratory setting to a spacious auditorium. When they went from the auditorium to the out-of-doors, their performance again improved. (Under each condition, matched comparison groups were used to control the practice effect.) Our subjects attributed their improved performance to the greater spontaneity and freedom they felt when using Exposé procedures in the more spacious setting.

Personal Exposé

This out-of-body procedure accesses precognitive information by either tapping into our subconscious sources of existing psychic knowledge or by "jump-starting" our dormant psychic mechanisms to produce totally new psychic information. Personal Exposé does not require astral travel to distant destinations.

The induction phase of the procedure requires a white screen which is viewed from a comfortable seated position. The screen, typically situated at a distance of about ten feet, provides a focal point that promotes relaxation and stimulates precognitive imagery. Here is the four-step procedure:

Step 1. Inducing the Out-of-Body State. To induce the out-of-body state, slow your breathing and clear your mind of all active thought by focusing on the white screen. After a few moments of focusing, close your eyes and envision your physical body at rest. Continue to envision your body resting peacefully until you sense yourself becoming separate from it. Stay with that sense of separateness, letting yourself gently float away from your body. Remind yourself that you are safe and secure. Invoke the protective power of higher astral planes, and using imagery, envelop yourself and your physical body in radiant white light. Tell yourself that you can return to your body at any moment you decide to do so. Let yourself feel free as you float farther away from your body. Affirm: *I am empowered and totally secure as I remain outside my body.*

Step 2. Accessing Precognitive Knowledge. Safely removed from your body, envision a white screen upon which appears a menu of precognitive topics. Appearing on the menu are a variety of topics, such as *Finances, Romance, Career, Travel,* and *Health,* along with any other topic you wish to add. Reserve one space on the menu for *General Information* to comprise precognitive information not covered by other topics. Select a topic from the menu and mentally "click" on it to call forth relevant precognitive information. Allow sufficient time for the information to emerge on the screen. You can call up the menu at will and continue "clicking" until you have the precognitive information you need.

Step 3. The Return. To return to your physical body, view it at rest and simply give yourself permission to re-engage it. Allow sufficient time for the return, then note your sense of physical presence, along with other specific sensations, such as areas of warmth or coolness.

Step 4. The Resolution. While remaining relaxed, take a few minutes to review the out-of-body experience and reflect on the precognitive information derived from it. Conclude the experience by affirming: *I am now empowered with knowledge of the future. I will use that knowledge wisely*.

Personal Exposé has many practical applications. An attorney who had been trained in Personal Exposé decided to use the procedure as an financial investment strategy. At Step 2, he clicked on *Stock Market* to call forth certain stock listings and their outlooks. He based his investment decisions on the predicted market values. The investment experts, who periodically evaluated the results of his investments, were stunned at the phenomenal success of his strategy.

Along a different line, an engineer used Personal Exposé to discover the love of his life. Upon reaching Step 2, he clicked on *Romance*, and immediately appearing on the screen was a woman he would meet for the first time at a social gathering the following day. The two were instantly attracted to each other and soon found themselves falling in love. Today, they attribute their unwavering "soulmate relationship" to cosmic intervention, not chance.

Personal Exposé is particularly useful as a career planning strategy. An undergraduate psychology student used the procedure to discover the graduate school he was later to attend. At the accessing step of the procedure, he clicked on *Education*, and immediately the name of a leading graduate school appeared on the screen. The school not only accepted his application for admission, but granted him a scholarship as well.

A victim of corporate down-sizing used Personal Exposé in his job search for a managerial position. At Step 2 of the procedure, he clicked on *Career*, whereupon the names of three regional corporations appeared on the screen. Assuming the corporations were listed in rank order of desirability, he focused his application efforts on the first corporation. Almost immediately, he was accepted for a top managerial position.

Cosmic Exposé

Cosmic Exposé, in contrast to Personal Exposé, requires out-of-body travel to distant astral realms in order to access higher sources of precognitive knowledge. The procedure is based on the notion that non-tangible dimensions of unrestricted knowledge exist in forms that are available to our out-of-body probes. Our conceptions of time, space, and reality can undergo expansive change when we enter those dimensions. Events yet to unfold in our known reality are often clearly visible in the astral realm. The information gleaned through this strategy ranges from the personally and globally relevant to the cosmically profound, unfolding either as sudden precognitive snapshots, or as a smooth progression of highly vivid, realistic images of the future. Here is the procedure:

Step 1. Induction. While seated comfortably, envision yourself surrounded by the glowing energies of the cosmos. Let peace and tranquillity infuse your total being. Envision a bright blanket of relaxation spreading slowly over your body, saturating every muscle and joint. Next, shift your attention to your forehead and focus on the inner region of light sometimes called the third eye. Continue to focus on that region as your link to higher astral planes. Finally, let the region of light in your forehead expand to infuse you fully and then ascend gently as the totality of your astral being, bearing consciousness away from your physical body.

Step 2. Out-of-Body Travel. With your astral being now disengaged from your physical body, you are empowered to travel safely to the distant reaches of the cosmos. As you scan the cosmos, you will notice a distant realm of light that commands your attention and invites your interaction. Sense yourself being drawn toward it, until finally you are at the center of it, encompassed by the light of cosmic power and knowledge. All that you need to know about the future is now available to you, taking shape before you as events spontaneously unfold. You can let yourself be drawn in as an active participant, or you can remain an objective observer. To access highly personal and detailed information, a simple question is sufficient.

Step 3. The Return. When your need for precognitive knowledge is satisfied, conscious intent alone is sufficient to initiate a return to your physical body. Upon gently re-entering your body, focus your attention again on the inner region of the third eye, now radiating light and energy. Affirm: *My total being is fully infused with the positive light and energy of the cosmos.*

Step 4. The Resolution. Take a few moments to review the precognitive experience, and reflect on its relevance and empowerment potential. Explore ways of using your precognitive knowledge. Remind yourself that cosmic predictions exist as probabilities, not as fate. For positive revelations, look for ways to facilitate the predicted outcomes. For negative revelations, consider ways of averting, altering, or preventing the predicted event. Bear in mind that even global catastrophes are not outside your sphere of influence when you are energized with cosmic knowledge and power.

Our laboratory studies of Cosmic Exposé over the past twelve years have documented an accuracy level for the procedure of approximately eighty percent. In addition to its effectiveness in predicting highly personal events, the procedure has accurately predicted many natural catastrophes, including hurricanes, volcanic eruptions, and earthquakes; and international crises such as revolutions, assassinations, and the rise and fall of political leaders.

At another level, Cosmic Exposé is valued as a strategy for probing higher spiritual dimensions and our destiny as spiritual beings. It can tap into astral planes beyond the realms of our known reality, and initiate highly significant interactions with them. Upon introduction to the *realm of light* in Step 2 of the procedure, spiritual teachers and guides with impeccable knowledge of the future often come forth.

In addition to the purely precognitive value of Cosmic Exposé, persons who routinely practice the procedure almost invariably experience important mental and physical health benefits. Healthful vitality, rejuvenation, and an increased sense of security and personal adequacy are among the strategy's positive spin-off effects. College students who routinely practice the procedure attest to its motivational value as well as its capacity to reduce anxiety, sharpen intellectual skills, and promote personal well-being. They report that simply lingering in the realm of light is enormously energizing and empowering.

The relationship between ESP and OBEs is one of the most challenging and potentially empowering frontiers of psychic study and research. As a fundamental expression of the self, ESP and OBEs alike call us out and beyond the dark and listless zone of mediocrity and into a bright dimension of enlightenment and new possibilities. The out-of-body state liberates our ESP faculties and manifests them as critical components of our astral being. The out-of-body state and ESP are, in fact, irrevocably linked. By exercising our out-of-body skills, we automatically develop our ESP faculties; by exercising our ESP faculties, we automatically develop our out-of-body skills. The result is a new level of cosmic enlightenment, attunement, and personal power.

5

OBEs and Psychokinesis

The whole visible world is only an imperceptible
atom in the ample bosom of nature.
No idea approaches it.

Blaise Pascal, *Pensées*

PSYCHOKINESIS (PK) IS the ability to influence material reality through sheer mind power. PK can, for instance, induce motion in a resting object or influence the velocity of a free-falling object. It can be deliberately applied to improve performance in a variety of physical activities, particularly in high-precision sports such as archery, billiards, and bowling. It can influence chemical reactions, the composition of compounds, the germination of a seed, and the rate of growth of plants—all of which have been observed in a controlled laboratory setting. In view of these discoveries, it should not be surprising to find that PK can also influence the functions of organs and systems in the biological body. On a massive scale, PK power could conceivably influence global conditions ranging from environmental pollution to natural catastrophes.

The critical first step in activating our PK faculty is a clear formulation of goals, followed by empowering imagery and positive affirmations of expected outcomes. Formulating and stating the PK goal makes it official. The process of verbalizing the goal alone is often sufficient to stimulate

PK, but with the introduction of relevant imagery and positive affirmations of expected outcomes, the PK faculty is further energized.

In the absence of specified goals, PK energies remain scattered and unfocused, except for certain situations in which the PK faculty is spontaneously activated and focused. Emergency situations involving danger, for instance, can elicit extraordinary feats of power in which our physical capacity is apparently exceeded by an urgent infusion of PK power. But even ordinary life situations can spontaneously evoke extraordinary PK powers, such as when we mentally slow the fall of an accidentally dropped object to prevent damage to it. PK can influence even the most fragile falling object to bounce rather than break.

The PK faculty, like our other psychic faculties, is energized and liberated by the out-of-body state. In out-of-body applications of PK, formulating PK goals prior to the out-of-body state places the PK faculty in a state of readiness and prepares it for easy activation. Once the out-of-body state is induced, the PK faculty operates independently of the physiological constraints that could otherwise impede its functions. With biological barriers minimized or banished altogether, our PK energies can become concentrated and directly focused to result in a forceful release of power.

The capacity for PK to influence physiology has critical health and fitness implications. In the out-of-body state, that capacity reaches its peak. The out-of-body state sets the stage for PK to target health needs, concentrate on specific biological organs or systems, and release powerful health energy.

The healing potential of OBEs can involve both *astral PK* and *PK channeling*. Astral PK is the power of consciousness in the out-of-body state to directly intervene into physiology to initiate the healing process. PK channeling, on the other hand, is the transfer of healing energy from a higher astral plane to produce desired biological change. Both concepts are similar in that they emphasize the healing power of consciousness in the out-of-body state. In astral PK, however, the healing process is consciousness-contained—that is, it remains a function of consciousness independent of distant astral planes—whereas in PK channeling, the healing process requires contact and interaction with the healing energies of a higher cosmic plane. The following OBEs procedures are based on these important concepts.

PK Pool of Power

When the goal of OBEs is health- and fitness-related, one of the most effective out-of-body procedures is the *PK Pool of Power*. This procedure introduces a crystal clear pool of astral healing energy. While in the out-of-body state, diving into the pool saturates our astral being with revitalizing energy, and spontaneously transfers mental and physical healing energy to the physical body at rest in the distance. Diving into the pool is supplemented by the *Chalice of Power*, a procedure used to take water from the pool and pour it over the astral body, further energizing consciousness and focusing its powers.

A period of approximately one hour should be set aside for the eight-step procedure to be conducted in a quiet, safe place. Here is the procedure:

Step 1. While resting in a comfortable, reclining position, with your legs uncrossed and your hands resting comfortably at your sides, take a few deep breaths, then develop a slow, rhythmic breathing pattern. Focus for a few minutes only on your breathing. Remind yourself that you are safe, comfortable, and secure. Invoke the empowering presence of higher astral influences by envisioning yourself surrounded by radiant light.

Step 2. Center your attention on your forehead, and slowly allow your thoughts to turn inward. Allow any darkness or shades of gray to become progressively brighter, until you experience only radiant white light. Envision your astral body as a radiant light form slowly rising from your physical body, and with it, your conscious awareness. As you rise above your body, notice your sense of freedom and serenity. You are at perfect peace as you ascend gently upward. Remind yourself that you are infused with light and protected by the highest influences of the cosmos. At any time, you can return to your body with ease upon deciding to do so.

Step 3. Now liberated from your biological body, you are free to travel wherever you decide to go. The distant reaches of the universe are now at your command. The highest dimensions and farthest planes invite your contact and interaction.

Step 4. As you sense a wondrous communion with the cosmos, turn your attention to a distant, crystalline plane glowing with pure energy. If you do not immediately identify the crystalline plane, continue scanning the cosmos until it comes into view, then let yourself be drawn to it. Upon entering the plane, you are immediately enveloped and invigorated by the warmth of its powerful energy.

Step 5. At the innermost region of the plane lies a crystal clear pool, calmly reflecting the sparkling radiance of the surrounding plane. Approaching the pool, you can sense the vastness of its power. Drawn by its amazing beauty, you plunge into the sparkling pool, probing its fathomless depths and limitless boundaries. As you explore the incredible pool, you sense a powerful infusion of invigorating energy.

Step 6. Upon ascending from the pool, you notice a beautiful, bejeweled chalice resting on a crystal pedestal at the pool's edge. Gazing in amazement at its intricate workmanship and exquisite beauty, you take the chalice from the pedestal and fill it with water from the pool. Upon lifting the chalice and pouring the water over your body, you are thrilled with fantastic pleasure as the water flows sensuously downward. Your total being is suddenly saturated with power. The vast riches of the universe are now at your command. Remind yourself that whatever you desire can now be yours.

Step 7. Now lifting the chalice toward the universe, affirm: *My thoughts and images are the language of the cosmos.* State your goals, envision them, and affirm them as present realities. If, for instance, your goals are health-related, state each goal specifically, envision the particular body part or system functioning normally, and affirm that the goal has been achieved.

Step 8. You are now ready to return the chalice to its place on the pedestal, and reunite with your physical body. Notice your body at rest and sense yourself gently re-engaging it. Upon re-entry and before opening your eyes, take a few moments to reflect on the experience and re-affirm its empowering effects.

The PK Pool of Power can be used for a wide range of health related goals. Among its many applications are fortifying the immune system and accelerating the body's natural healing processes. A very high success rate has been reported by men and women who used the procedure to slow the aging process. Also in pain treatment programs, the procedure has been highly effective, not only in managing pain but in promoting healing as well. In drug treatment programs, the procedure has been used successfully to build self-esteem, reduce stress, and promote a general sense of personal empowerment.

Astral PK Strategy

The *Astral PK Strategy* is designed to empower us to muster our inner PK resources while in the out-of-body state and focus them on specific health and fitness goals. This approach, which does not require travel to higher cosmic planes, differs somewhat from other strategies in that the astral body retains the structural features and dimensions of the physical body, but in astral form. As a non-biological copy or double of the physical body, the astral body provides a complete model with specific astral parts that parallel the physical body and its biological parts. Such an astral double serves two important functions: First, it permits a focused concentration of healing energies on specific astral parts, and second, it promotes an easy transfer of those energies to specific biological counterparts. The healing rationale of these functions holds that if a weak or defective organ or system in astral form is energized and repaired, the same organ or system in biological form is also energized and repaired, in at least two ways: 1) by the immediate transfer of healthful astral energy during the out-of-body state, and 2) by the later re-engagement of the empowered astral body with the biological body. Here is the procedure:

Step 1. Statement of Goals. Formulate your health goals by affirming your objectives and creating mental images of the desired outcomes. For instance, if your goal is to be full of energy and to enjoy life more, envision yourself engaged in your favorite activities with your body aglow with health and vigor. If your goal is to repair a damaged body organ, envision the organ glowing with vitality and functioning normally.

Step 2. Induction. Astral PK combines three elements—relaxation, imagery, and affirmation—to induce the out-of-body state. Once your physical body is fully relaxed, give yourself permission to disengage it, and afterward, to remain in close proximity to it. Sense your astral body becoming separate from your physical body but remaining near it in the form of a glowing aura of energy that replicates it. (At this point, the astral body is typically experienced as hovering closely over the physical body.)

Step 3. Astral Infusion. Now apart from your biological body, focus on the parallel astral parts or systems to be energized, and saturate them with radiant energy. Mentally engage your biological body at rest, and infuse the counterpart organs and systems with powerful astral energy. Energize you total being, both astral and biological, with powerful energy.

Step 4. Astral Return. The infusion process now complete, initiate astral return by affirming your intent to re-unite with your biological body. Sense the reunion process, paying particular attention to the powerful merging of specific astral and biological organs and systems. Once re-engagement is complete, you will experience a final burst of powerful energy that fills you totally—mentally, physically, and spiritually.

Step 5. Conclusion. Review the experience and mentally re-infuse your body with healthful vigor. Again, mentally saturate specific organs and systems with positive energy, then affirm: *I am at my peak of empowerment.*

Along with its many other uses, Astral PK has been used to accelerate recovery from a wide range of sports-related injuries. It is particularly effective in the treatment of muscle and joint injuries. Some athletes use the procedure routinely to prevent injury by infusing the physical body with protective astral energy prior to practice, workout, or competitive events.

PK Channeling Strategy

Through the *PK Channeling Strategy*, we can personally experience higher astral planes and draw healing energy from them to infuse either our own physiology or that of others. Although the healing effects of astral channeling are typically gradual in nature, they can also be instant and complete.

Healing through astral channeling is based on the notion that certain astral planes or astral entities are primary sources of pure cosmic healing power. When we tap into those sources, we can draw from their healing resources and channel them to specific biological targets. OBEs are possibly the most direct way to access and channel the healing powers of higher planes and entities.

In the laboratory setting, experimental subjects practicing astral channeling reported *deep emerald green* as the color that typically characterized the astral plane associated with healing. When an emerald gem, or simply the imagery of an emerald, was incorporated into the procedure, induction was accelerated, and the emerald green plane was more readily accessed. As a footnote, the emerald is believed by many psychics to possess healing and rejuvenating properties, or at least to have physical frequencies that are attuned to cosmic healing energies. Tending to confirm that belief are the scientific surveys that show the emerald to be the gemstone of choice among centenarians.

Following are the seven steps of PK Channeling:

Step 1. Formulate your goals and state them as specific expectations. Use imagery whenever possible to envision the desired end results.

Step 2. Settle back and let yourself become comfortable and relaxed, then verbalize your intent to enter the out-of-body state and to access higher sources of healing. Envision yourself enveloped in light, secure and protected by the power of higher astral planes.

Step 3. With an emerald (or if no emerald is available, an imaginary emerald) resting in either hand, close your eyes and focus on the innermost region of your being. Allow any area of darkness to give way to emergent light, until you are totally infused with positive energy.

Step 4. To enter the out-of-body state, form a clear image of consciousness as a light form gently rising from your physical body, which remains in a state of deep rest. Allow adequate time for the out-of-body state to emerge, then affirm: *I am totally protected and secure as I travel out-of-body to the distant realms of the cosmos.*

Step 5. With consciousness disengaged from the biological body, envision an iridescent cosmic plane of emerald green, radiating with healing energy. Allow the plane to become clearly visible, then give yourself permission to ascend to and interact with it.

Step 6. Upon entering the plane, probe its innermost regions and draw from its concentration of healing energy. With yourself now fully infused, project healing energy to your designated biological target.

When your own physical body is the target, focus on the astral cord of energy connecting you to your biological body resting at a distance, and use the cord as a channel to transport radiant healing energy. During channeling, the typically glowing astral cord will take on added brilliance. Allow channeling to continue until your physical body radiates powerful healing energy. Select as needed specific biological organs or systems and infuse them with radiant healing energy.

When your designated target is another person, envision that individual and, if known, their present physical location. Imagine a dynamic channel of energy connecting you to that person, and use it to transport healing energy from the emerald green astral plane. Envision your target subject infused with glowing health and vitality. Whenever required, focus on specific body regions of your subject and saturate them with healing energy.

NOTE: At this step, an out-of-body visit can be used to supplement the PK channeling process. Healing out-of-body visitations are recommended only after an abundant supply of astral healing energy has been gathered. The out-of-body visitation is designed to transport the accumulated energy and transmit it to the receiving subject. The accumulated energy can be imparted through *out-of-body aura massage,* in which the recipient's surrounding aura is energized by gentle astral strokes. This process requires a consenting subject who is receptive to the procedure.

Step 7. To end the out-of-body experience, turn your attention to your physical body at rest and give yourself permission to return to it. Allow a few moments for astral-biological re-engagement to occur, then focus on various physical sensations. Notice the emerald (real or imagined) in your hand, and allow it to radiate vitality through your being. Form images of particular body parts, and saturate them with healing energy. Conclude the experience with the affirmation:

> I am infused with health and vitality. I am empowered to unleash abundant healing energy by envisioning the emerald which represents my contact with the healing energies of the cosmos.

In addition to its application in promoting general health, PK Channeling has been effectively used to achieve highly specific health goals. A sixty-eight year-old woman who was stricken with arthritis experienced a dramatic remission of her condition following her participation in an experimental program that included out-of-body aura massage. The massages were conducted daily over a period of two weeks, after which they were conducted once weekly for a period of four weeks. Over the six-week period, the out-of-body massages were supplemented weekly by conventional aura massages, in which the aura around the affected body areas was gently massaged using circular motions, but in the absence of any physical contact with the body. For the duration of the program, the subject was advised to wear an emerald pendant and, while periodically holding it in her hand, to envision her body enveloped in healthful energy. At the end of the six-week period, she was free of the pain and swelling that had plagued her for many years. Periodic follow-up contacts occurred over the next several months, during which she continued to wear the emerald pendant, and reported no recurrence of symptoms.

Out-of-body PK is yet another example of the empowerment possibilities of OBEs. Our capacity to use our PK faculties in the out-of-body state reflects the astral nature of this powerful phenomenon. Since our PK powers are operational during the out-of-body state, it would follow that we could retain that same capacity in the discarnate state. The possibility of discarnate intervention into our present physical reality, consequently, becomes a reasonable expectation, with enormous empowerment implications.

6

OBEs and Sleep

Even sleepers are workers and collaborators
in what goes on in the universe.

Heraclitus, *Fragments*

S INCE WE SPEND about a third of our lives in sleep, it is not surprising
that spontaneous OBEs often occur during that altered state of consciousness. Many of our so-called "dream experiences" seem clearly to
meet the criteria for OBEs. In fact, many experts hold that sleep itself is an
out-of-body state with the astral body disengaged from the physical body,
but typically remaining in close proximity to it for the duration of the
sleep period. According to this view, the various stages of sleep as measured physiologically, including *rapid eye movement* (REM) sleep, are
merely biological concomitants of OBEs without clearly defined cause-
effect relationships.

Although the relationship between observed physiological changes during sleep and OBEs remains unclear, our laboratory studies suggest that
certain physiological changes, including REM sleep, do seem to signal, if
not trigger, OBEs. It is during the REM stage of sleep that the *broken-corona*
effect, which has been found to characterize the out-of-body state, is typically observed in the electrophotographs of sleeping laboratory subjects
who, upon awakening, reported having had OBEs. The broken-corona

effect is not observed among sleeping subjects who did not report OBEs upon awakening. (See Chapter 10 for further discussion of electrophotography and the broken-corona effect.)

The sleep state is believed to be conducive to out-of-body travel for several reasons. Whether or not we accept the notion that sleep itself is an out-of-body state, the biological body during sleep is typically in a relaxed, restful state, one of the essential conditions for astral disengagement. Also, the psychological state of the sleeping subject is typically peaceful and passive, conditions that further facilitate the slipping away of the astral from the physical body. Finally, the environmental conditions of sleep are usually conducive to the out-of-body state.

Spontaneous OBEs during sleep often include travel over familiar terrain, visits to distant destinations, and occasional interactions with acquaintances who are also in the out-of-body state. Many spontaneous out-of-body interactions during sleep seem to be motivated by intimacy needs. A college professor traveling abroad reported a "dream-like" out-of-body visit with her husband, who was at the time also out-of-body. During the visit, they caressed, and after sharing intimate moments, discussed several happenings of the previous day, including the professor's purchase of a jade art object and her husband's minor fender-bender. On the following day, a call from her husband verified the out-of-body visit. He confirmed the fender-bender and inquired further concerning her purchase of the art object.

Spontaneous OBEs during sleep often involve specially meaningful interactions with higher cosmic planes. Examples are visits with astral entities, including loved ones who have crossed over to the other side. These spontaneous interactions can be an important source of insight, as well as comfort in times of grief.

Numerous strategies have been developed specifically to promote easy out-of-body travel during sleep. Among the most effective of these strategies are *Transitional Travel* and *Astral Flow*. Both procedures capture the transitional stage of falling asleep and progress into the sleep state itself.

Transitional Travel

Transitional Travel is designed not only to facilitate easy out-of-body travel during sleep, but also to give greater control of the out-of-body experience. Here is the five-step procedure:

Step 1. Preparation. Just before falling asleep, relax your entire body by mentally scanning it and releasing all tension. Focus on slowing your breathing. Suggest to yourself that time is slowing down.

Step 2. Affirmation. Affirm that, as you sleep, you will slip out of your body and travel to a distant destination. Selecting a specific destination is optional. Invoke higher plane protection and the empowering presence of ministering guides by affirming: *I am fully protected and secure as I travel out-of-body*.

Step 3. Mental Imagery. Form a clear image of your astral body as a vaporous form rising from your physical body as sleep ensues. In that projected state, view your physical body at rest enveloped in a protective glow, and allow your astral being to float further away from your body.

Step 4. Astral Travel. Flow spontaneously into distant realities, or travel deliberately to a predetermined destination. For specific destinations, envision the destination and re-affirm your intent to experience it. Give yourself permission to gain knowledge and power from the experience.

Step 5. Re-entry. Conclude the astral adventure by returning at will to rejoin your physical body. At this point in the procedure, you may choose either to awaken from sleep or to allow sleep to continue uninterrupted.

Astral Flow

Astral Flow is a laboratory-tested method designed to arrest sleep and induce out-of-body travel to distant physical as well as astral realities. The procedure begins with a mind-clearing exercise to extinguish active thought and introduce a positive state of well-being. Next, a state of inner harmony is generated through inner-focusing strategies, and finally, sleep is delayed as imagery and suggestions are used to induce the out-of-body state. Here is the five-step procedure:

Step 1. OBEs Conditioning. In a peaceful, relaxed setting free of distractions, settle back and affirm your intent to travel out-of-body as you sleep. Clearly specify your objectives. If possible, enrich your stated objectives with visualization, including images of the outcome of the out-of-body experience.

Having formulated your objectives, free yourself of all active thought by envisioning your mind as a room with an open window through which your thoughts, as puffs of vapor, can pass freely and then vanish. Continue this exercise until your mind is emptied of all worries, problems, and concerns. Should unwelcome thoughts enter your mind, do not respond to them. Rather, let them become vapor-like images that move away from you and disappear through the open window. Note a sense of renewal and well-being as your mind becomes cleared of active thought.

Step 2. Inner Harmony. Center your full attention on your breathing. Breathe in and out effortlessly and naturally. You will note a sense of harmony and oneness with your body as you continue to focus only on your breathing. At this moment, only your breathing is important. Pay attention to nothing else. After a short period of concentration, you will become fully absorbed in the wondrous inner world of your existence. You are, at that point, at perfect peace with your total being. Imagine peace as radiant energy infusing your body and enveloping your total being with a white glow. Continued focus on this process will lead to increased relaxation and drowsiness.

Step 3. Sleep Arrest. As drowsiness ensues, arrest sleep by spreading the fingers of either or both hands. While holding the spread position, focus your attention on a magical garden in the cosmos with a magnificent central fountain. Notice bright marble steps leading up to the stately fountain with its spray glistening in the light. Holding your vision of the splendid fountain, invoke the protective presence of higher astral powers, then gradually relax your fingers as you find yourself slowly slipping away from your body.

Step 4. The Journey. With your fingers now fully relaxed, and your physical body in a state of restful sleep, give yourself permission to travel out-of-body to the cosmic garden. Focus again on the enchanted garden and yourself ascending the marble steps leading to its central fountain. Now in the fountain's presence, let yourself become energized by its splendor and radiance. You can further empower yourself by stepping into the fountain's glistening spray, allowing your total being to fully absorb its radiant energy.

To travel beyond the fountain, re-affirm both your intent and your objectives, and then envision your destination. Infused and protected by white light, you will sense yourself leaving the fountain behind, slipping upward and away toward your destination. Once at your destination, engage it in an empowering interaction appropriate to your stated objectives.

Step 5. The Return. Upon achieving your out-of-body objectives, you may permit other out-of-body travel to occur spontaneously, or you may choose to end the travel experience by focusing again on the fountain and allowing yourself to return to it. Once in the fountain's presence, envision your body at rest, and then let yourself slowly return to its familiar setting. At this point, you may wish to remain disengaged from your physical body as sleep continues uninterrupted, or you may decide to reunite with it. Should you decide to awaken from sleep, simply give yourself permission to reunite with your body, and then turn your attention to your breathing and other physical sensations. Conclude the procedure by reviewing the out-of-body experience and re-affirming its empowering effects.

During your visit to the fountain in Step 3, you can adapt the procedure to meet your health and fitness needs. By stepping into the fountain's spray, you can energize your body, mind, and spirit with health and renewal. You can direct the fountain's energy to specific biological organs and systems, infusing them with glowing vitality. You can draw from the fountain's rejuvenating powers to either slow or, in some instances, totally arrest aging. By lingering in the fountain's spray of healing energy, you can fortify your body's immune system, restore normal functioning to your biological organs and systems, and create a state of inner harmony. To maximize these health benefits, numerous visits to the fountain may be required, but the empowering results are well worth the time and effort. What better way to spend one's sleeping hours?

Aside from its physical health applications, Astral Flow has shown considerable promise as a mental health strategy. It has been particularly effective in the treatment of sleep disturbances, such as insomnia and breathing-related sleep disorders. It has also been useful in the treatment of anxiety, obsessive-compulsive, and depressive disorders, including conditions with suicidal ideations. This unique procedure taps into our wealth of inner health resources as well as the immeasurable healing potential of higher astral planes.

Astral Flow illustrates a critical psychic empowerment principle: Any application of OBEs to empower any part of our being will invariably promote our total well-being. Consequently, when we intervene into our biological system to promote our physical well-being, we indirectly promote our mental well-being, and vice versa. The following chapter examines out-of-body strategies that were specifically developed for use in counseling and psychotherapy. The empowering effects of these strategies, however, are all-encompassing. They permeate our entire being— mentally, physically, and spiritually.

7

OBEs in Counseling and Psychotherapy

Nowhere can man find a quieter or more untroubled retreat than in his own soul.

Marcus Aurelius

I N THE PSYCHOTHERAPY setting, spontaneous OBEs with important therapeutic implications often occur, typically with approaches using techniques such as hypnosis, cognitive relaxation, biofeedback, or meditation.
These techniques—manifestations of consciousness—reflect our inner
striving to expand our awareness and knowledge beyond the borders of
common sensory experience. The liberation of consciousness from its biological constraints opens a wondrous cosmic gateway to new dimensions
of enlightenment and growth.

In recent years, numerous therapeutic out-of-body strategies have
been developed and are currently being used by counselors and psy-
chotherapists who recognize OBEs as a potential source of personal
empowerment. Even skeptical mental health professionals who question
the phenomenon admit that OBE-like experiences do occasionally occur
spontaneously among patients undergoing therapy. Increasingly, contemporary therapists of various orientations are recognizing the empowering
value of these experiences and are using out-of-body strategies in their
therapy programs.

OBEs, possibly more than any other human experience, put us in touch with the master therapist within each of us. OBEs can access our inner resources and activate them to enrich our lives. They can empower us to solve pressing problems, resolve distressing conflicts, achieve crucial personal goals, and actualize our highest potentials. At another level, they can energize and empower us to tap into the therapeutic resources of higher astral planes. Through the out-of-body experience, all the healing resources of the self and the universe become available to us.

Out-of-body therapy is an integration of three critical elements: 1) the incomparable worth of each human being; 2) the capacity of the mind to heal itself; and 3) the matchless power of higher astral planes. Each of the following procedures is designed to empower our lives by accessing and activating our dormant inner potentials, while drawing on the rich resources of higher planes of power.

Astral Plane Therapy

Astral Plane Therapy is based on the concept that simply experiencing higher astral planes is inherently therapeutic. Even in the absence of clearly formulated goals, this strategy energizes and empowers by spontaneously generating positive feelings of security and self-worth. It can be structured, however, to achieve highly specific therapy goals, such as overcoming depression, reducing anxiety, and breaking unwanted habits, to name only a few. In the group therapy setting, the procedure has been remarkably effective in generating positive interactions and building productive relationships.

A comfortable, reclining position is recommend for Astral Plane Therapy. This procedure requires approximately one hour in a setting free of distractions. Here is the process:

Step 1. Body Scan. With your eyes closed, mentally scan your body and relax each muscle, beginning at your forehead and progressing downward. When the scan is complete and your body is relaxed, focus your full attention on your breathing. Continue focusing on your breathing until it develops a slow, rhythmic pattern.

Step 2. Out-of-Body Induction. With your body now fully relaxed, envision yourself so liberated from the pressures of life that you begin to drift gently upward like a white vapor, away from your physical body, leaving all your cares behind. Notice the sense of freedom and wondrous release from your body, which is now at rest below you.

Step 3. Affirmation. As you remain suspended over your body and enveloped in radiant light, affirm: *I am now balanced, energized, and at peace with myself and the universe.* Mentally invoke the power of the higher astral planes and notice the colorful concentrations of pure cosmic energy slowly emerging from a distance and surrounding your astral body. Think of each color as representing a particular cosmic resource, such as green for good health, blue for tranquillity, and yellow for enlightenment. Allow each colorful concentration to permeate your whole being. Notice the forceful infusion of positive energy. Allow yourself to remain in this quiet, unencumbered state until your entire being is saturated with power.

Step 4. Astral Travel (Optional). At this step, astral travel may occur either spontaneously or voluntarily as you remain enveloped in bright astral energy.

Step 5. Re-engagement and Re-affirmation. Gently re-engage your physical body by first viewing it at rest, then deliberately descending and settling into it. Before opening your eyes, focus again on your breathing, and affirm, *I am now fully infused with abundant energy and power.*

Astral Plane Therapy has been particularly effective in couples therapy for resolving conflicts. A couple whose marriage was disturbed because of career pressures, discovered the therapeutic value of Astral Plane Therapy in overcoming the barriers in their relationship. Guided by their therapist, the couple simultaneously entered the out-of-body state, and in Step 4, they visited a tropical island of indescribable beauty together. Strolling hand-in-hand on an isolated beach, they explored their feelings in a relaxed Caribbean setting. As homework, they set aside a time for therapeutic out-of-body strolls on the beach, after which they would discuss the experience and share their feelings. On one such astral visit, they had out-of-body sex under a tropical full moon, an experience that proved to be the turning point in their relationship. In the weeks that followed, they continued their out-of-body visits to the familiar island, particularly during periods of protracted separation. Their out-of-body interactions empowered them to strengthen their relationship and eventually resolve the conflicts that had threatened to destroy it.

Although primarily designed for use in the mental health setting, Astral Plane Therapy has been used effectively in a variety of other situations. A group of performing artists who experimented with the technique reported significant improvements in their working relationships and performance on stage. In the athletic setting, the technique has been used with remarkable effectiveness as a team motivational strategy. Along another line, a university student running for office in student government used the procedure with his campaign workers to build a winning spirit. Calling the procedure *higher plane meditation*, he attributed the outstanding success of his campaign effort largely to the strategy that, in his words, put "new life into the campaign."

Several specialized OBEs procedures have been developed in recent years for use in treating a wide range of highly specific disorders. Among the most useful of these strategies are those designed to extinguish phobias. Although numerous conventional psychotherapy procedures are available for the treatment of phobias, they are not always effective, particularly for those persistent, irrational fears that are acquired early in life or appear to be related to past-life trauma.

The out-of-body state provides the ideal conditions for extinguishing fear. With our biological functions at rest, and the physiological correlates of fear, such as a pounding heart and shortness of breath, effectively controlled, we are psychically empowered to face our fears and overcome them. Of equal, if not greater, significance are the resources of higher astral planes that offer the support system so essential to the out-of-body treatment of phobias.

Two out-of-body procedures, *Astral Regression Therapy* and *the Crystalline Sphere Technique*, have demonstrated remarkable effectiveness in treating phobias, including those that resist extinction when conventional approaches are used. Both procedures emphasize disownership of the phobia, while recognizing its existence and negative effects. Either procedure can be used with or without the assistance of a trained therapist.

Astral Regression Therapy

Astral Regression Therapy is structured specifically to extinguish deep-seated fears, including phobias that emerge suddenly full-blown. Using this procedure, we can re-experience the events and conditions that gave rise to the phobia, without the distress that originally accompanied the experience. A single session is often sufficient to extinguish even the most intense phobia.

The procedure requires approximately one hour in a quiet setting, free of distractions. A comfortable, reclining position is recommended. Here is the procedure:

Step 1. Preliminary Considerations. Prior to using the procedure, clearly formulate your therapeutic goals. Specify in as much detail as possible the events and conditions that gave rise to the phobia, and envision them as your regression destination. (If the origin of the fear is unknown, the destination can be specified simply as the phobia's *point of origin.* Although unknown to conscious awareness, the origins of fears are known to our higher consciousness and can be revealed during the out-of-body state). Formulate a *therapeutic plan* including: 1) regressing out-of-body to the point of origin of the fear and, 2) extinguishing the fear by re-experiencing, in a secure, empowered state, its point of origin.

Step 2. OBEs Induction. To induce the out-of-body state, follow Steps 1 and 2 of Astral Plane Therapy as previously presented.

Step 3. Astral Flight. Formulate a clear image of your out-of-body destination, and give yourself permission to travel to it. Envision yourself surrounded by radiant, empowering energy, and affirm the therapeutic presence of higher astral guides. Reject all ownership of the fear as you affirm:

I will be guided and protected by the illimitable power of higher astral planes as I travel to the origin of the fear that has plagued my life. I will face the fear, uproot it, and toss it out of my life. (Notice that personal ownership of fear is rejected through the reference, "*the* fear" rather than "*my* fear.")

Center your full attention on your destination until you are consciously aware of being there. If the destination is unknown, rely on your ministering guides or your higher self to guide you to it. A few moments are usually sufficient to reach even the most distant location. Once at your destination, focus your attention on your surroundings.

Stage 4. Destination Activities. At this critical step, implement your previously formulated therapeutic plan. It is important to remain at the destination until the complete plan has been fully implemented. The therapeutic activities are concluded with affirmations such as:

> *I am fully empowered and free of fear and its disempowering effects on my life. I now disown the fear that has plagued my life. I will no longer be a victim of it. I am the master of my life and my destiny.*

Stage 5. Astral Return. Once you have implemented your destination plan, shift your attention back to your physical body at rest and give yourself permission to return to it. Once in the presence of your body, allow yourself to slip gently back into it. Once re-engagement is complete, affirm:

> *I have achieved my goal of complete liberation from fear. I am confident, secure, and fully empowered.*

Astral Regression Therapy was used by a psychotherapist to help a college student who had experienced a frightening out-of-body experience that appeared to be the source of a persistent fear of heights. By the student's account, the fear originated when he spontaneously entered the out-of-body state for the first time about a year earlier. Upon becoming drowsy while studying in a reference room on the third floor of the university library, he became overwhelmed by fright when he suddenly found himself drifting to a window and viewing the sprawling campus below. His fear intensified even further when he felt himself uncontrollably slipping through the window. Inexperienced in managing OBEs, and after several frustrated attempts to return to his physical body, he was finally able to re-engage it, only to experience a full-blown fear of heights. The phobia was so intense that he immediately avoided all heights, and discontinued attending classes except those meeting on the first floor. Eventually, he sought therapy for the condition, which had seriously interrupted his academic progress.

In the safe therapeutic setting, the student, after being oriented about the therapeutic potential of OBEs, consented to use the procedure. He was reassured of his ability to leave his body and safely return to it. A destination plan was formulated, and he consented to travel out-of-body to the library reference room and re-experience the conditions that gave rise to the phobia. He was provided appropriate out-of-body travel instructions that included the use of intent and imagery, first to direct the flight experience to the desired destination, and second, to return safely to his physical body on command.

Armed with these instructions, and secure in his ability to use the procedure, he calmly entered the out-of-body state and almost instantly traveled to the familiar reference room setting. Upon approaching the window, he again focused on the campus below, not with fright but rather with bold confidence in his ability to overcome the fear of heights. Momentarily lingering at the window, the fear disappeared as suddenly as it had appeared. Before returning to his body, he adventurously traveled out-of-body beyond the window and above the campus, fully liberated from the fear that had hounded him for many months.

The Crystalline Sphere Technique

The *Crystalline Sphere Technique* is an out-of-body procedure specifically designed to explore past-life influences and extinguish painful, unresolved past-life issues, particularly fears associated with past-life trauma. Past-life enlightenment is inherently empowering and therapeutic. Simply uncovering the past-life sources of our fears is often sufficient to totally extinguish them and instantly stimulate new growth.

The Crystalline Sphere Technique is based on our analysis of the spontaneous OBEs of persons whose phobias were counteracted by simply re-experiencing the past-life origins of their fears while in the out-of-body state. Approximately one hour should be allowed for the procedure, which is conducted in a quiet setting, free of distractions with the subject resting in a comfortable, reclining position. Here is the procedure:

Step l. Preliminary Considerations. Before inducing the out-of-body state, formulate your goals as specifically as possible. Examples are: *I will use OBEs to discover any past-life source of the fear that has troubled my life.* (Note the reference to "the fear" rather than "my fear," thus disowning the phobia while recognizing its existence and distressing effects.)

Step 2. OBEs Induction. Induce the appropriate out-of-body state by applying Steps 1 and 2 of Astral Plane Therapy as previously presented.

Step 3. Crystalline Encasement. While remaining suspended over your physical body, surround yourself with radiant astral energy by envisioning yourself safely encased in a protective, crystalline sphere. Affirm:

> *I am protected and empowered mentally, physically, and spiritually by the highest forces of the cosmos. As I travel to higher astral planes, I will remain encased in a powerful cosmic sphere of energy. I will be accompanied by astral guides who will shield me and direct my flight.*

Step 4. Experiencing Higher Astral Planes. At this step, the ascent to higher planes is initiated by envisioning the astral realm with its bright array of planes. From this point, allow the astral journey to unfold under the direction of higher guides as you remain encased in the crystalline sphere. (Many out-of-body travelers report that the cosmic sphere not only functions as a space travel craft, it amplifies the empowerment frequencies of higher astral planes as well.) Once you arrive at your astral destination, therapeutic interactions can occur within the crystal sphere under the direction of astral teachers and guides. The sphere may, on the other hand, open up to permit very direct, therapeutic interactions outside the sphere.

Step 5. Experiencing the Origin of the Fear. With the help of higher astral guides, you are now empowered to experience relevant past-life events, either as realistic projections on the inner surface of the crystalline sphere, or as an active participant outside the sphere in an astral re-creation of the past events. Experiencing your past at this step of the procedure is like participating in an exciting theater production under the direction of skilled specialists. Although facing the origins of our fears, even in the company of caring guides, can be at first painful and disturbing, the resulting enlightenment and liberation can be permanent and profound.

Step 6. Re-engaging the Biological body. Your return to the physical body, like other steps of the procedure, is helped by the ministering guides who are accompanists throughout the experience. Once in the presence of your body, slipping from the astral sphere and back into your physical body is typically smooth and effortless. Upon re-uniting with your body, note the serenity permeating your being, then affirm:

> *I am fully empowered and free of fear. My life is enriched and constantly energized by the limitless resources of the higher cosmic planes.*

At first glance, the Crystalline Sphere Technique may seem quite complex, but once the conducive out-of-body state has been achieved, and once the sphere of astral energy has been formed, the remainder of the procedure usually unfolds effortlessly in the caring presence of ministering guides.

A college student with complaints of claustrophobia used the Crystalline Sphere Technique to clear up a traumatic past-life experience related to the fear. Encased in the crystalline sphere and accompanied by a familiar ministering guide, he traveled to a plane of radiant beauty and came to rest among several astral beings arrayed in shining robes. He sensed an immediate affinity for the gathering that encircled the crystalline sphere.

As he remained safely inside the sphere, a series of images that he immediately recognized as reflections of past lives were projected on the sphere's inner surface. He immediately recognized each flashing scene on the concave screen as a significant remnant of a past life. Eventually, vivid images of his own past death in an avalanche of snow appeared on the screen. He saw himself overwhelmed with panic, struggling to escape the frigid capsule that imprisoned him. His frantic efforts only compacted the snow more solidly around him, until he could no longer move or breathe.

Suddenly, the past-life source of his claustrophobia was clearly evident. In a flash, he felt afresh the utter panic and terror of the past experience. Then amazingly, as the projected images slowly disappeared, his fear gently faded, leaving behind only peace and calm. Finally, a powerful infusion of positive energy from the circle of astral entities filled him totally as he remained safely enveloped in the crystalline sphere.

Upon reuniting with his physical body, he again experienced a powerful surge of energy and full release of his past-life baggage. Incredibly, this single out-of-body experience permanently liberated him from the pain and bondage of a life-long fear.

Although designed specifically to extinguish fear, the Crystalline Sphere Technique is a highly flexible procedure that can be easily adapted to explore a wide range of past-life experiences. The procedure's essential elements—the crystalline sphere, higher astral planes, and ministering astral guides—provide a highly interactive structure for personal empowerment through past-life enlightenment.

Sexual Interchange Strategy

An innovative OBEs procedure specifically designed for use in partners therapy is *Sexual Interchange*, a form of out-of-body sexual interaction involving temporary gender reversal. The procedure is particularly effective in strengthening intimate relationships and overcoming barriers to sexual fulfillment; it can, however, evoke considerable anxiety, particularly for the insecure partner who may experience ambivalence in the gender reversal stage of the procedure. More than sex-role reversal, gender reversal reassigns the biological gender of each partner through an astral "walk-in" technique in which the partners concurrently engage the biological body of the other partner. Although sensuously exciting during the temporary gender exchange, latent sexual impulses and repressed memories, along with gender-identity conflicts, can surface, and homophobic reactions can occur. The potentially disempowering effects of these responses, however, can be minimized by open discussions before and after the procedure.

The potential empowering benefits of Sexual Interchange far outweigh any risks that may be inherent in the procedure. The strategy has valuable potential for those seeking insight into, and resolution of, identity and relationship conflicts. The approach is highly effective in overcoming various sexual dysfunctions, such as inhibited orgasm, sexual aversion, and sexual arousal disorders. In some instances, a single sexual interchange experience is sufficient to restore full sexual functioning.

Sexual Interchange requires approximately one hour in a private setting with no distractions. Here is the strategy:

Stage 1. Preliminary Considerations. At this stage, the interchange partners, having already been introduced to the procedure, engage in open discussion, in which they share their deeper feelings and concerns. The complete consent of both partners to practice the procedure in private is critical to its success.

Stage 2. OBEs Induction. Having mutually consented to practice sexual interchange, the partners concurrently induce the out-of-body state as they lie comfortably together in close proximity, but without physical contact. For induction, Steps 1 through 6 of OBEs Levitation as presented in Chapter Three are recommended. Since partners often find that they achieve the out-of-body state at different rates, sufficient time must be allowed to assure that both partners are in the out-of-body state. Experienced partners will sense the mutual emergence of the out-of-body state.

Stage 3. Astral Embrace. Once a mutual out-of-body state has been achieved, the partners engage in an astral embrace while suspended over their physical bodies which remain comfortably at rest below them.

Stage 4. Gender Exchange. At this critical point in the procedure, each partner first envisions, then astrally engages, the biological body of the other partner. In the male-female dyad, the astral male assumes a female biology while the astral female assumes a male biology, resulting in a gender reversal state which we could call *out-of-one's-own-body-but-in-the-body-of-the-other*. Because they are outside their own bodies, the partners, while temporarily possessing the physical body of the other partner, remain in the astral projected state. Periodically throughout the procedure, imagery of the possessed body may be required to maintain the gender reversal state.

Stage 5. Interchange Arousal. While in the projected, gender reversal state, with each partner in possession of the other's body, the partners engage in sexual foreplay, typically through erotic expressions involving physical touch as well as mental and verbal communication. As sexual arousal emerges and throughout the ensuing sexual interchange, the gender reversal state is carefully maintained.

Stage 6. Sexual Interchange. With the female partner in astral possession of the male body, and the male partner in astral possession of the female body, sexual interchange as a *combined form of astral and physical intercourse* is initiated. The sexual interchange experience typically culminates in mutual orgasm.

Stage 7. Interchange Resolution. Following sexual interchange and while retaining the out-of-one's-own-body-but-in-the-body-of-the-other state, a period of reflection and relaxation is recommended, during which the partners share feelings and thoughts concerning the experience.

Stage 8. The Astral Embrace and Return. At this stage, the partners simultaneously engage in a brief period of quiet relaxation, then exit each other's body by intentionally shifting astral awareness above the two physical bodies which remain at rest and in close proximity. While in that levitated out-of-body state, the partners embrace, after which they re-engage their own physical bodies. Each partner then focuses attention on the physical body and its various sensations.

Stage 9. Post-Interchange Embrace and Resolution. The partners conclude the sexual interchange experience by physically embracing and again sharing their innermost thoughts and feelings.

A major advantage of Sexual Interchange as a psychotherapy technique, aside from its direct empowering effects on relationships, is its capacity to put us in touch with the other side of our sexuality. Our genetic makeup—including the pairing of chromosomes that determine our gender—consists of equal contributions from each of our parents. Through Sexual Interchange, men and women alike can discover the empowering potential of their total sexuality—including their masculine and feminine sides. Men who practice the technique experience greater appreciation of their feminine side, and women who practice of the technique report greater appreciation of their masculine side. The result is a healthful balance between our feminine and masculine sides, and a better understanding of the other sex. Equally as important, Sexual Interchange reveals that men and women are actually more alike than they are different. Whatever our physical, cultural, social, and psychological differences, we are, first and foremost, human beings, and we are of the same planet.

Aside from its psychotherapeutic value, Sexual Interchange has shown amazing promise as a fertility empowerment procedure. In one remarkable instance, a couple turned in desperation to Sexual Interchange after two years of failed efforts using advanced fertility techniques. The result was a prompt pregnancy. In another amazing instance, a husband, who had been advised that he was sterile, used the procedure with his wife to result in a pregnancy that produced fraternal twins.

Although numerous case records indicate the remarkable efficacy of Sexual Interchange as a fertility procedure, the underlying dynamics and complex interactions involved in the procedure remain largely unknown. Sexual Interchange seems to set into motion the intricate psychological, astral, and biological functions that facilitate pregnancy. From an interactive perspective, the couple's astral bodies, once interchanged, could energize their biological reproductive systems while stimulating a mental state conducive to pregnancy. On the other hand, the procedure could simply evoke our psychokinetic powers that, in turn, directly target and activate dormant reproductive functions. Yet another view holds that Astral Interchange is essentially a rejuvenation procedure that literally reverses the aging process and increases sexual potency. This view would explain the procedure's success with older couples whose reproductive clocks had slowed down or expired.

In this chapter, we have examined only a few of the therapeutic applications of OBEs. With OBEs moving firmly into the field of counseling and psychotherapy, we are left with three compelling conclusions. First, a master therapist who is unsurpassed in therapeutic skill exists within each of us and is ready to act in our behalf; second, abundant resources with infinite therapeutic potential exist in the astral dimension and are readily available to us; and third, OBEs are invaluable therapeutic vehicles that can connect us to these inexhaustible sources of growth and well-being.

8

OBEs and Past-Life Experiences

All the past is here, present to be tried.

Henry David Thoreau, *Journal*

A T THE EPICENTER of our existence is the indestructible part of our being we call the *higher self*. It spans our existence from our earliest beginnings to the present and beyond. It is our point of contact with distant cosmic sources of knowledge and higher astral planes. It is endowed with the advanced skills of a creative teacher and master therapist. When attuned to the cosmos, it guides our growth and energizes our lives with the resources required to achieve our highest goals. It resides within the very soul of our being.

A major goal of OBEs is increased awareness of the higher self through a phenomenon known as *cosmic illumination*. Cosmic illumination helps us understand the larger cosmic scheme of our existence while empowering us with deep insight into ourselves. Through cosmic illumination, we become more attuned, both to our own being and to the outer cosmos. Cosmic illumination challenges us to master our lives and shape our own destiny.

Cosmic illumination is a never-ending process of growth and discovery. Awareness of our past-life experiences is critical to that process. But as incarnates, the more we learn about ourselves and our past, the less, it seems, we know. In the life-after-life or discarnate realm, however, cosmic illumination rapidly accelerates through a process known as *discarnate illumination*. In that dimension, we are progressively empowered through discarnate illumination to use our past-life experiences as critical growth resources.

The ultimate goal of discarnate illumination is *cosmic actualization,* in which the growth potential of our past-life experiences is finally realized. As discarnates, we are then ready either to return to this earth plane to gather more growth experiences or to ascend to other cosmic levels and roles. Assisting in that transition process are other discarnate luminaries and ministering entities. Some highly advanced discarnate luminaries choose to return to this earth plane, not only to accelerate their own development, but also to promote the growth of others or to achieve goals of global significance.

Fortunately, discarnate illumination, while essential in after-life, is not limited to our development in the discarnate realm. It is an essential component of our present growth and enlightenment. Our evolution, in both the present and after-life, demands the raw material of experience. The wider our background of experience, the greater our potential for wisdom and power.

Critical to our present and future growth is expanded awareness of our cumulative past history and the magnitude of our experience in three critical dimensions—*pre-incarnate, incarnate,* and *discarnate*. Our *pre-incarnate history* is a record of our existence prior to our first incarnate lifetime. Our *incarnate history* is the record of our past lifetimes as incarnates on this earth plane. Our *discarnate history* is the record of our personal existence in the discarnate realm between past lifetimes and following our final incarnation. Together, these three dimensions of personal experience form the totality of our existence as a conscious entity in the cosmos.

Incarnate consciousness exists on a *continuum of awareness*, with certain restraints always in place. For instance, many of our past experiences exist within the self as stored memories, but our efforts to retrieve them are often unsuccessful. In contrast, discarnate consciousness seems to exist on a *continuum of attentiveness*, in which we have conscious command of our past experience on a "need-to-know" basis. In the discarnate state, "everything can be everywhere all the time." That is to say, we can be wherever we need to be, and have command of whatever we need to know at the moment. Regulating that unfolding phenomenon are the higher self and higher plane entities, including our ministering guides.

From the psychic empowerment perspective, *reincarnation* is a developmental phenomenon on an endless growth spiral. The concept of reincarnation emphasizes the indestructible nature of the individual as a conscious entity, while recognizing the wisdom, splendor, and eminence of higher astral planes. It provides a comprehensive structure for viewing the richness and fullness of our existence, including our many lifetimes and the critical developmental intervals between them. Reincarnation manifests the continuity of our development and our intimate, unseverable connectedness to the cosmos.

Reincarnation, not death, is the great leveler of humankind, because it empowers each of us, lifetime-by-lifetime, to eventually realize our peak potential at our own growth rates. As individuals, our growth patterns vary. The person whose growth is rapid will gather in a given lifetime more growth experiences and make more quantum leaps than the person whose growth is slow or thwarted. Additional lifetimes can compensate for these differences. From the cross-cultural perspective, each culture offers growth options that differ significantly from other cultures, thus affecting the growth rates and opportunities available to its members. Lifetimes in other cultures equalize the experience, expanding awareness and growth.

Historically, lessons to be learned in one time period may not be available in another. Participating in many civilizations at different periods of history assures a greater accumulation of direct and varied experience. We can, of course, acquire knowledge of past civilizations through the study of historical records. But knowledge gained retrospectively of the past is a poor substitute for active participation and first-hand experience in the real world of unfolding events. Multiple lifetimes at different places and times dramatically increase our store of knowledge, as well as our appreciation of the past.

With today's information explosion and unprecedented technological advancements, reincarnation is increasingly relevant in our quest for knowledge and enlightenment. Today, with the World Wide Web in place, we have access to more information than ever before, and can access it more quickly. (The "downside" to downloading, however, is the problem of cyberspace junk and content credibility.) But even under state-of-the-art learning conditions, we could not, in a given lifetime, acquire the total knowledge or master all the skills associated with even a single field of study. Successive lifetimes, while not ensuring mastery, would unquestionably increase our command of accumulated knowledge while promoting our personal evolvement.

Aside from its personal relevance, reincarnation has significance on a global scale. We are imperfect participants in an imperfect world. Individually and collectively, we have created the planet's problems, and the planet is now repaying us, with interest. We have carried into the present the baggage of our past on a global scale. Fortunately, the accumulated karmic debts amassed from our past lifetimes are offset by the empowering potential of our past learning. Through awareness of our past, and recognition of the decline we have set into motion, we increase our capacity to intervene and reverse the downward spiral of personal and global disempowerment. Knowledge gained in past lifetimes, if retrieved, could be applied in today's world to enrich the quality of life on this planet and solve widespread problems, such as war, poverty, prejudice, and suffering—all of which impede our personal and global progress.

Urgent global conditions are not unique to contemporary life—each era seems to create its own crises. However, periods of crisis can be cosmically foreseen, and they may require cosmic intervention, including the reincarnation of experienced, empowered leaders for the express purpose of shaping global destiny. Many global advancements may be the result of cosmic intervention that introduced enlightened leaders and reformers specifically to bring humanitarian change to the world.

Reincarnation reflects the cumulative nature of our existence. From our pre-incarnation to the present, we are the product of all that we have experienced. Unfortunately, our life experiences are not always positive and empowering. We can, for instance, acquire prejudices or other negative dispositions that resist change, dominate our lives, and thwart our growth. If the resources we carry to the discarnate side, and our experiences in that dimension, are insufficient to reverse our acquired negative traits, we may require another lifetime to eradicate them. Not infrequently, a life as a persecutor is followed by a life of humanitarian service and commitment to human rights. Our past-life regression studies of people in the helping professions often reveal past lives as despots, and even executioners.

The familiar saying, "What goes around comes around," has at least limited application to reincarnation. Incarnate experience is often the best teacher, and in some instances, it seems to be the only alternative. Notwithstanding the growth resources we take with us to the other side and the opportunities offered there for our continued growth, we may require another incarnation to expiate guilt, overcome a destructive impulse, or correct a wrong. A life of misuse of power or reckless indulgence, for instance, may require a follow-up life of subordination and service. Only through incarnate experience can we eradicate some of the deep past-life imprints that resist change in the discarnate state.

Along a more positive line, reincarnation is often characterized by empowering continuity from life to life. More than one life may be required to complete an important task, or to fulfill a dream. Many lives are cut short by accident or early death, leaving behind a void of interrupted relationships and strivings. Reincarnation opens the door for us to resume progress and renew our relationships, often with even greater satisfaction. This was strikingly illustrated by a psychiatrist who lost his father in a traffic accident. With the later birth of his son, the psychiatrist almost immediately noticed traits of his father—subtle gestures, a familiar smile, a certain look, and later, certain verbal expressions that had been unique to his father. It became increasingly clear to him that his son was, in fact, the reincarnation of his father. The renewed bond with his father, now his son, was validated by a past-life regression that not only uncovered a long history of past lives together, but also revealed a spirit guide who had remained with both over several lifetimes, a phenomenon that is almost always evident in successive lives characterized by strong bonds.

In our reincarnation studies, many of our subjects discovered that they had returned again and again to renew their temporal bonds with another person while developing together as soulmates and pursuing their common goals. Common to these soulmate relationships was a spontaneous, mutual awareness of their past-life roles and experiences together.

Although soulmates typically contribute to the evolution of each other, they can also limit our capacity to pursue other roles and relationships. Our analyses of soulmate relationships occasionally revealed subtle approach-avoidance conflicts, in which the need to maintain the relationship conflicted with the need to establish other close relationships, particularly when the soulmate relationship was romantic in nature. Personal insight into the nature of soulmate roles and relationships is consistently empowering to both partners. It increases the spontaneity of the relationship, while liberating each partner to pursue other goals and fulfill other growth needs.

The goals of reincarnation are always progressive. Many reincarnations seem to be specifically structured to re-direct our growth and flex our adaptive muscles by initiating totally new roles and relationships in unfamiliar settings. Reincarnation cuts across all cultures and socioeconomic strata. Reincarnation often modifies biases learned in one lifetime by introducing the appropriate counter-conditions in another lifetime. For example, a person's prejudice toward a particular socioeconomic or subcultural group can be effectively extinguished by a future lifetime as a member of that group. On a broader scale, several lifetimes in markedly different cultures can make us more tolerant of the vast differences found among cultures on our planet. The result is raised global consciousness and freedom from the karmic baggage that so often impedes our progress.

Elitism, ageism, sexism, and prejudice are learned patterns of behavior that resist change, even in the discarnate state. Fortunately, these disempowering patterns, even when deeply ingrained, willingly yield to *reincarnation reversals* that expose their destructive nature. In reincarnation reversal, a past-life role, characteristic, or activity is reversed in a later life. A common example is gender reversal. For the male, a future reincarnation as a female can shatter his gender stereotypes and increase his acceptance of his feminine side. Similarly, for the female, a future reincarnation as a male can generate new insight and promote her acceptance of her masculine side. The frequency of past-life gender reversal is probably about the same for both men and women; however, in our regression studies, very few male subjects admitted having been female in a past life, a phenomenon that may be due to subtle cultural conditioning, particularly in cultures that assign women an inferior role, or in cultures characterized by a long history of discrimination against women.

At a very practical level, reincarnation has important implications for career development. Most of us spend a major part of our lives in career pursuits or career-related activities. Individually, however, we have multiple interests and aptitudes that qualify us for success in a wide range of careers. Although on average we make around three major career changes in a given lifetime, many of us, at an early age, make irreversible career choices that lock us into a career track for life and thus limit our growth options. Reincarnation offers new opportunities for achievement and fulfillment in a variety of new career fields.

Through *past-life retrieval procedures*, we can often uncover the subtle, yet powerful, influences that have shaped our career choices and pursuits. Our retrieval studies revealed that we seldom pursue the same career in successive lifetimes. We may choose nursing in one lifetime and carpentry in another, or politics in one lifetime and teaching in another. Through pursuing one life-long career, we discover not only its benefits but its limitations as well. That awareness may push us toward a different career choice in a future life. On the other hand, career pursuits that are cut short, or career needs that are thwarted, may motivate us to continue a particular career in a future lifetime. One of the few careers that tends to repeat itself from lifetime to lifetime is medicine. Past-life regression of medical doctors often reveals their frustration with the limitations of medicine in a past life, thus motivating them to pursue medicine in a later life using improved approaches and advanced technology.

The primary goal of past-life retrieval is to lift our awareness of our past-life experiences, particularly those with growth potential and relevance to our present-life strivings. But while knowledge of our past is itself empowering, acquiring the prerequisite skills and mastering the strategies required for retrieving that knowledge are of equal, if not greater, importance. The skills required to access our past lives are easily transferable and can be readily adapted to access other important information sources. The foundation of all psychic accessing strategies, including past-life retrieval, is an unwavering need for knowledge. By mastering a single empowerment strategy, or even a simple component of a complex strategy, we increase our repertoire of empowerment skills, while directly stimulating our overall evolution.

At the conscious level, we have varying degrees of awareness of our past experiences, including those related to our past lifetimes. Some of these experiences are immediately available and easily accessed, whereas others require considerable effort to uncover. If we could master the skills required to retrieve critical insight from our past, we could possibly dissolve our present growth barriers and appreciably accelerate the rate of our evolution. Once empowered with knowledge from our past, we can more directly maximize our potential, while resolving any negative residue from our past.

Many of our present-life experiences are so far removed from conscious awareness that they require specialized retrieval strategies, the most popular of which is *hypnotic age regression*. Age regression is a phenomenon in which the individual, typically during hypnosis, recalls or re-lives past experiences lost to present memory. The use of hypnosis as a memory retrieval strategy is based on the Freudian premise that within the self exists a storehouse of repressed or "forgotten" past experiences called the *unconscious*. Although buried in the unconscious, these repressed experiences continue to influence our behavior, often in disempowering ways. Only when the self's defensive or repressive mechanisms are relaxed or removed can the multitude of experiences buried in the unconscious be resurrected and brought forth into conscious awareness. Given increased awareness and insight into our past, we become empowered to resolve conflicts and cope with the stresses of the present. An extension of this view holds that not only many present-life experiences, but mountains of past-life experiences as well, are submerged in the vast unconscious, and can be retrieved, and in some instances re-experienced, through hypnosis—a phenomenon called *past-life regression*.

Hypnosis is an altered state of consciousness in which our concentration is focused and our receptivity to suggestion is heightened. A major concern of specialists in the field, however, has been the accuracy of hypnosis as a retrieval strategy. Among the major problematic factors are the "leading questions" frequently posed by the hypnotist, along with the subject's often obvious need to please the hypnotist and meet his or her expectations, particularly when the hypnotist is also the subject's psychotherapist. Also problematic are the discrepancies and apparent "false memories" that all too often characterize the hypnotic accounts of past happenings. Forensic specialists agree that even eyewitness accounts immediately following an event are often inconsistent from witness to witness, and obviously inaccurate when compared with the hard evidence.

In view of these findings, none of us would be comfortable with crucial judgments of guilt or innocence based solely on evidence gathered by hypnosis. Hypnotic evidence, like eyewitness accounts, is always stronger when corroborated by evidence collected through other strategies.

Nevertheless, past-life regression through hypnosis, while needing further research, remains an important strategy for gathering information about past lifetimes, as well as the nature of human existence in the discarnate intervals between lifetimes. Fortunately, hypnosis is only one of numerous strategies with potential for exploring the past. Dreams, for instance, often reveal elements of past lifetimes, and some dream states are almost identical to the discarnate or in-between-life state described by a hypnotized subject during regression. Similarly, certain illuminating "peak experiences" can transcend our awareness and reveal glimpses of other dimensions, including past lifetimes. Finally, the near-death experience—one of the most profound of all human experiences—often engages a panoramic view of past lifetimes along with transforming interactions with higher planes. (For a further discussion of these and related phenomena, see *Psychic Empowerment: A Seven Day Self-Development Plan* and *Psychic Empowerment for Health and Fitness.*)

Often undervalued, or overlooked altogether, is the capacity of OBEs to access the past, including past incarnate and discarnate life. The out-of-body state, in some ways, parallels the discarnate state itself. In both states, consciousness continues, with certain spontaneous regulatory mechanisms still in place. These mechanisms control the recall of past experiences, while activating the growth potentials related to them. In both states, the emergence of past experiences occurs only at the pace we can accommodate.

OBEs can accelerate our growth by either introducing totally new growth experiences, or by retrieving past experiences and activating their dormant growth potentials. As already noted, memories lost because of physical and psychological trauma often unfold during the out-of-body state. With our biological systems—including the central nervous system—in a state of rest, past memories and their positive growth capacities are often unleashed. But potentially harmful memories are spontaneously screened from awareness until we are ready to profit from them. Given permission of the higher self and the assistance of our ministering guides, those memories that we can accommodate and which are important to us at the moment can come forth clearly and free of distortion in the out-of-body state.

The lessons we learned in previous lifetimes are cumulative and always relevant to present-life tasks. With increased awareness of the past, we become more fully empowered to shape the future and achieve our highest goals. Awareness of past successes can generate a success expectancy effect that is self-fulfilling. Awareness of past failures is likewise important, because it not only reveals what did not succeed, but often suggests more workable alternatives.

Past-life retrieval efforts can yield important information of therapeutic value. Phobias, as previously noted, are often associated with unresolved past-life trauma. Awareness of the traumatic experience alone is often sufficient to fully extinguish the phobia. In another vein, personality disorders—particularly obsessive-compulsive, histrionic, antisocial, and narcissistic disorders—have dynamics that strongly suggest past-life influences that are affecting our present growth. Similarly, the factors associated with drug abuse frequently point to personal predispositions and other influencing factors that reach into past lifetimes. Given awareness of the past-life experiences associated with these conditions, we become more effective in breaking down the barriers and resolving the conflicts that thwart our growth. Past-life enlightenment, rather than providing an excuse for our problems, challenges us to engage with them, and find solutions.

Hypnotically Induced OBEs

OBEs and past-life regression are phenomena often experienced spontaneously during hypnosis, particularly when *hand levitation* is used to induce the trance state. Hypnotic induction through hand levitation seems to precede more generalized sensations of weightlessness followed by out-of-body impressions as the trance state deepens. Subjects who spontaneously enter the out-of-body state during hypnosis almost invariably report sensations of physical weightlessness preceding the actual disengagement of the astral body from the physical body. They often report impressions of full physical levitation which appear to be, in fact, astral levitation. Only when they view the physical body at rest below them do they become aware of the out-of-body state.

Although OBEs and past-life regression often occur spontaneously and independently of each other during hypnosis, they can occur together. When regression occurs during hypnotically induced OBEs, awareness of past-life experiences is typically more vivid and detailed than in hypnotically-induced regression independent of the out-of-body state. This may be due to the fact that both hypnosis and the out-of-body state are highly conducive to past-life regression. Consequently these two states of consciousness, when combined, generate an optimal condition for past-life enlightenment.

Past-life Ascent

Because the hypnotically induced out-of-body state appears to be the ideal condition for past-life regression, we developed a procedure called *Past-Life Ascent* which uses both hypnosis and the out-of-body state to retrieve past-life experiences and glean empowering knowledge from them. This procedure holds that the records of our past are astral rather than biological in nature. Consequently, past-life regression becomes an astral phenomenon, with the resulting past-life enlightenment due to raised consciousness.

Past-Life Ascent views past life as a three-dimensional phenomenon: Pre-incarnate life is our existence prior to our first incarnation; incarnate life is our existence as incarnates in each lifetime; and discarnate life is our existence as discarnates between lifetimes.

Past-Life Ascent is a comprehensive strategy consisting of three critical components: 1) hypnosis, 2) the out-of-body state, and 3) cosmic ascension. This unique procedure is a positive, empowering approach that recognizes the power of consciousness in the ascended, out-of-body state to comprehend the totality of our past and access the latent growth potentials found there.

The goal of Past-Life Ascent is *cosmic ascension* rather than *past-life regression*. Cosmic ascension is an altered state of raised out-of-body consciousness in which past-life awareness reaches its peak. A major advantage of Past-Life Ascent over regression approaches concerns the superior wisdom and perceptual accuracy of the ascended out-of-body state. In Past-Life Ascent, rather than *regressing* into the past, we *ascend* to a higher cosmic level, from which our past can be viewed with greater clarity and understanding.

Past-Life Ascent offers a sweeping overview of all our past experiences, from the earliest to the present. In that cosmically elevated state, specific past lifetimes can be retrieved and reviewed in as much detail as needed, and with greater objectivity. The emotional experience of regressing to actively re-experience a past-life event, particularly when the event is painful, can distort the experience and interrupt the healing functions of the higher self. By experiencing past-life events in the ascended state, we not only accommodate them more effectively, we can integrate them in ways that invariably raise our consciousness and facilitate our growth. As it turns out, cosmic ascension is both enlightening and therapeutic. It is, in fact, one of the most advanced and empowering forms of human expression.

Past-Life Ascent is based on the premise that past-life experiences are recorded on two levels: 1) *personal consciousness* and 2) *cosmic archives*. Personal consciousness is a complete inner chronicle of our life experiences, including our pre-incarnate, incarnate, and discarnate existence. The cosmic archives are the comprehensive records of the cosmos, which subsume our personal archives. Consequently, the evolution of our personal consciousness becomes an integral part of a greater cosmic process. These two dimensions of archives are suggested by the Biblical metaphor of tangible records found in Revelation 20:12, "...and *the books* were opened, and *another book* was opened, which is the book of life...." (emphasis added). Here *"the books"* represent the totality of cosmic history and *"another book"* represents the chronicle of our personal consciousness.

The vast inner record of our past-life experiences is often not easily retrieved, because of memory limitations, biological constraints, or various regulating or defense mechanisms—such as denial, resistance, distortion, and repression. Consequently, our conventional attempts to retrieve past-life experiences through direct strategies, such as hypnosis, are often thwarted. Even when the inner barriers to retrieval are recognized and bypassed through more indirect procedures, such as free association, projection, automatic writing, and dream analysis, subconscious material typically surfaces only in disguised, fragmented, or other cryptic form. Furthermore, our interpretation of that material is typically subjective and highly speculative. Past-Life Ascent, rather than being designed to overcome the inner barriers to past-life recall, is designed to directly access the higher cosmic archives and the personal records found in them.

Through Past-Life Ascent, we can experience the full scope of our personal existence on a cosmic scale. We can discover the cosmic nature of our personal consciousness, and a new congruency between ourselves and the cosmos. The technique reveals not only relevant past-life experiences, but, whenever pertinent, forgotten aspects of our present life which are being progressively entered into the cosmic record of our existence.

Past-Life Ascent unveils three dimensions of cosmic archives that together reflect the extensive span of our existence, from our earliest beginnings to the present. The first dimension, *pre-incarnate archives*, contains the records of our existence before our first lifetime on the planet Earth. The second dimension, *incarnate archives*, contains the records of our experiences in each incarnation, including not only our past lifetimes but our present lifetime as well. The third dimension, *discarnate archives*, contains the records of our experiences between lifetimes. Together, our pre-incarnate, incarnate, and discarnate archives offer an inexhaustible source of knowledge. Each past-life ascent provides an empowering view of our existence and lifts our consciousness to a new level of cosmic enlightenment.

While the underlying dynamics of Past-Life Ascent may at first seem complex, the procedure itself is easily mastered with even limited practice. It requires no trained hypnotist other than yourself to induce the trance state. Since you know yourself best, you alone are your own best hypnotist. In the strictest sense, all hypnosis is self-hypnosis, since in the absence of a consenting, responding self, the trance state will not occur. You alone possess the inner capacity to experience and understand the totality of your personal existence, from your distant pre-incarnate existence to your present incarnation. The innermost part of our being is an enthusiastic collaborator in all our efforts to know the deepest meanings of our existence, and only the self is empowered to validate these efforts.

Like other out-of-body procedures, Past-Life Ascent requires a quiet, comfortable setting. Approximately one hour during which there are absolutely no interruptions should be set aside for the session. Here is the six-step procedure:

Step 1. Goal Formulation. Formulate your personal objectives and state them as specifically as possible. Your objectives may simply be to practice the procedure and develop your induction skills. On the other hand, you may wish to conduct a comprehensive overview of your past lives, or to investigate a particular past lifetime in-depth. Your goal may be to explore past-life experiences that relate to a particular present situation, or to identify past-life themes or patterns, such as recurring relationships, careers, or commitments. You may wish to explore past-life tasks you can now complete, or past-life problems you can now solve. You may decide to explore your earliest pre-incarnate existence, or certain discarnate intervals between your past lives. You may wish to identify your most recent past lifetime, or to re-experience your very earliest incarnation. You may decide to explore your past-life experiences in a given geographic region or within a particular culture. Your goal may be to discover important knowledge gained in a previous life but presently lost to conscious awareness. You may wish to explore your past experiences concerning a present problem or objective. If, for instance, you are faced with problems in your personal relationships, a deeper understanding of your past-life relationships could offer insight and suggest possible solutions. Or if you are experiencing conflict regarding a career decision, awareness of your past-life career experiences could be an invaluable source of occupational information.

Step 2. Trance Induction by Hand Levitation. Having formulated your objectives, settle back into a comfortable, reclining position with your legs uncrossed and your hands resting on your thighs. With your eyes closed, mentally scan your body from your head downward, releasing all tension as you go. Upon completing the scan, take a few deep breaths, exhaling slowly. Develop a comfortable, rhythmic breathing pattern, counting backward with each breath from ten to one.

Upon completing your backward counting, continue breathing rhythmically as you focus your full attention on your hands resting on your thighs. Note specific sensations, such as warmth, tingling, numbness, and the slight pressure of your hands on your thighs. After a few moments of concentration, center your full attention on your right hand and imagine it becoming weightless. Imagine a gentle force under your hand, slowly pushing it upward toward your forehead.

As your hand rises gently, give yourself permission to enter deep hypnosis and then, to leave your body. With your hand steadily rising, affirm:

When my hand touches my forehead, I will enter a deep hypnotic trance. Upon relaxing my hand and allowing it to return slowly to my thigh, hypnosis will give way to the out-of-body state. Upon leaving my body, I will be fully conscious, safe, and secure. I will be enveloped and protected by the powerful energies and guiding forces of higher cosmic planes. I will return to my body at any moment by simply deciding to do so. Upon returning to my body, I will exit hypnosis by simply counting from one to five.

Allow plenty of time for your hand to levitate until it touches your forehead, then affirm:

I am now in hypnosis and prepared to leave my body by simply relaxing my hand and allowing it to slowly resume its original position.

Let your hand now slowly return to its position on your thigh.

Step 3. Astral Disengagement. With your hand now resting on your thigh, sense yourself gently leaving your body and rising slowly above it. You can facilitate the disengagement process by simply envisioning your astral body as a glowing mist lifting quietly from your biological body and remaining suspended over it. Once in the out-of-body state, view your biological body as it remains in a passive state of rest. Sense the powerful radiance enveloping your total being, then affirm:

I am now outside my physical body, fully enveloped by pure, radiant cosmic energy. The radiance enveloping my astral being extends to my biological body, protecting and energizing it as I travel to higher astral planes. The highest realms of the cosmos are now receptive to my interactions.

Step 4. Cosmic Ascension. At this crucial stage of the procedure, the goals are twofold: first, to ascend to the realm of cosmic archives known for its bright hub of light and sweeping swirls of radiant color, and second, to access cosmic sources of past-life experiences. Cosmic ascension is typically accompanied by awareness of special astral guides who are almost always enveloped in luminous violet energy. The presence of guides is invoked by affirmations of your intent to ascend astrally and acquire relevant past-life knowledge. Suggested affirmations include the following:

*I am now prepared to ascend to the realm of cosmic archives in
my efforts to gain new insight and knowledge concerning my past.
I now invoke the empowering presence of astral guides who will
be my constant companions throughout this experience.*

The ascension experience is typically characterized by sensations
of being gently carried forward, first through darkness and then into
radiant, fluid-like dimensions of varying coloration. Certain dimensions appear as planes of color with many concentrations of light;
whereas others emerge as light-filled corridors or channels of energy.
During ascension, awareness of time and space is often replaced by
a raised state of cosmic awareness which spontaneously guides consciousness into the archival center of cosmic knowledge.

As ascension progresses, you will recognize in the distance a
magnificent hub of light with outward spirals of multicolored lights.
This luminous core of cosmic energy emits an endless radiance
manifesting the creative power of the cosmos. Once in the hub's
field of influence, you will experience its gentle attraction, drawing
you slowly into its central region. The approach to the cosmic core
is invariably accompanied by expanded awareness of oneness with
the universe. No longer simply an astral traveler, you are now an
integral part of the cosmos, interconnected and interacting with its
limitless knowledge and power.

Upon entering the bright cosmic hub, you will notice the surrounding multicolored lights forming a great wall consisting of
many side-by-side *vertical frames* within which unfolds your past in
chronological order, from your pre-incarnation existence to your
present incarnation. Each vertical frame represents a significant
period of your past, with the first frame depicting a record of your
pre-incarnate existence, and each successive frame depicting either
a lifetime or a discarnate interval between lives. Pictured in each
frame is a progression of your growth, beginning at the bottom of
the frame and culminating at the top. The last frame, which is
incomplete, is a record your present lifetime.

As your past unfolds before you in discrete vertical frames, you
will notice the continuity and common themes of your life. The
total cosmic span of your past, including each cosmic frame and its
complete contents, is now at your command.

Commanding your attention are certain highlighted contents that represent significant events or turning points in your evolution. Guided by the higher wisdom of the cosmos, you can allow the frames to progressively unfold, or you can arrest certain frames, download specific contents, including those highlighted, and focus on their empowering relevance.

It is important to emphasize the confidential nature of cosmic archives. The cosmic records of each individual are available to that individual alone.

Step 5. Astral Return. To end the ascension experience, affirm your intent to return to your physical body which is resting comfortably at a distance. Sense again the presence of your escorting guides, who are now poised to accompany your return and guide your re-entry. Upon re-engaging your physical body, the hypnotic trance is spontaneously resumed.

Step 6. Resolution and Conclusion. Allow the hypnotic trance to continue as you briefly reflect on the ascension experience, then affirm:

> Upon ending this trance state by counting from one to five, I will have immediate and full recall of all that I experienced during my out-of-body ascension. I will understand the significance of this experience, and use the knowledge gained from it to enrich and empower my life.

As you count from one to five, intersperse your counting with suggestions of increased alertness.

Conclude the procedure by further reflecting on the ascension experience and contemplating its relevance. Give particular attention to the events that commanded your attention, and the common threads that characterized your past-life history.

In our laboratory studies, comparisons of past-life regression using *hypnosis only* versus Past-Life Ascent revealed greater consistency for the latter from session to session, not only in the information acquired concerning a particular past life, but in the scope of individual past-life records. Multiple Past-Life Ascents can build a reasonably complete past-life history which not only chronicles past lives but also examines the intervals between them. Such an effort, however, usually requires careful documentation, in the form of a *past-life journal* which details the results of each session.

Analysis of the cosmic ascension journals of our subjects often revealed recurring themes that spanned their cosmic histories. For instance, the past-life histories of some subjects were characterized by artistic interests, whereas others were characterized by scientific pursuits. A progressive unfolding of certain personal traits and the tendency for unfulfilled strivings to pass from one incarnation to the next were frequently noted in past-life histories. Also noted were frequent soulmate relationships, which not only recurred from life to life, but also continued during discarnate intervals. Past-Life Ascent, while typically validating the long-term nature of soulmate relationships, also revealed that such relationships can originate during a given incarnation as well as during a discarnate interval. Soulmates in the discarnate realm often wait until both partners were ready before beginning another lifetime together.

Almost without exception, soulmate relationships were found to be complementary in nature, with each soulmate contributing to the development of the other. Perhaps not surprisingly, current soulmate relationships are almost always accompanied by a strong, mutual awareness of the past-life origin of the relationship.

On average, Past-Life Ascent subjects found an overall upward growth spiral characterizing their past developmental histories. A major recurring theme in their ascension experiences was their capacity to use their acquired strengths to compensate for their weaknesses. Although growth setbacks occurred in almost every lifetime, they were specific to certain areas of growth only, and were typically overcome later in life. But at times, the growth spiral was so severely interrupted—often by overwhelming adversity or trauma—that resolution during that lifetime was not possible, thereby presenting a discarnate challenge to overcome the growth deficits of the past life. These barriers to growth, if not removed in the discarnate realm, were typically re-introduced as growth challenges in the next incarnation. We were surprised to find, however, that flaws and growth barriers carried into the discarnate realm were sometimes "set aside" at the time of the next incarnation, only to be interjected later, during either a discarnate interval or a future incarnation. Under the counsel of teachers and guides, very serious setbacks were sometimes held over several reincarnations before they were again introduced for resolution, a procedure apparently regulated by the subject's own state of "cosmic readiness." Although our accumulated deficiencies, flaws, conflicts, and traumas will be eventually overpowered, they must occasionally be held back in our personal archives until we develop the specific skills required to master them. For our subjects, growth barriers never originated in the discarnate realm; however growth challenges were often introduced there, where they were met successfully with the assistance of astral guides and teachers.

Certain recurring gender patterns were often found among our subjects over the history of their past lives. Occasionally we noted intriguing ratios of gender reversal—such as two incarnations as female followed by one incarnation as male throughout a given individual's span of past lives. Only rarely did gender seem random, or remain unchanged over a past life history.

Antithesis—in which a growth phenomenon or life role is reversed in a following incarnation—was occasionally noted in our subject's past-life histories. For instance, a lifetime of deprivation is often followed a lifetime of enrichment, and vice versa. Perhaps predictably, a lifetime characterized by strong prejudices against a particular group was often followed by a lifetime of membership in that group. This phenomenon was illustrated by a Jewish student, who discovered during Past-Life Ascent that he had held strong prejudices against Jews in his last incarnation. In a remarkable instance of antithesis, a student whose father had disowned him because of his sexual orientation discovered that he himself had disowned his own son in a previous lifetime for the same reason. Past-life ascension subjects almost always recognize the growth benefits of antithesis, and willingly embrace instances of it in their personal past-life histories. The complexity and brilliance of antithesis, along with many other ingenuous phenomena seen throughout the universe, suggest a cosmic intelligence of matchless splendor at work within a cosmic "master plan" of immeasurable scope.

Analysis of the past-life journals of our subjects revealed an extensive range of highlighted contents in their cosmic archives. Highlighted contents were found in all past-life records, including both incarnate and discarnate life frames. Many of these highlighted contents occurred during childhood, a finding that underlines the critical importance of early experiences in our future development. Interestingly, the highlights found in past-life histories seldom involved temporal achievements, such as wealth and fame; they focused instead on the enlightening effects of phenomena such as moments of illumination, transformation, and peak experiences.

Among the major advantages of Past-Life Ascent is its capacity to explore the continuity and progressive nature of our evolution, beginning at the pre-incarnate stage. Almost without exception, ascent subjects viewed their pre-incarnate experiences as critical to their future development. In multiple Past-Life Ascents for a given subject, the pre-incarnate accounts would be highly consistent, with almost no discrepancies. Also, comparisons among subjects revealed strong similarities and common elements in their pre-incarnate accounts. Highly positive descriptions, such as *filled with the brightness of love, complete peace*, and *a gentle, nurturing presence,* typically characterized their reports. They were unanimous in their conclusions that the pre-incarnate state was a period of growth and progressive enlightenment in which ministering angels, teachers, and guides were present, along with other pre-incarnate entities and discarnate luminaries. According to our ascent subjects, certain pre-incarnates were more highly advanced than discarnates who had lived many lives. Our subjects attributed this phenomenon to the unique capacity of certain pre-incarnates to learn from their teachers and guides, as well as vicariously through advanced discarnates. According to our subjects, many higher plane teachers and guides had no direct incarnate experience.

Our ascension subjects discovered that their existence between lives was similar to their pre-incarnate existence, but with certain distinct advantages—the most important being the enriching effect of past-life experiences on the earth plane. These experiences became the raw materials for discarnate growth—which was, for the most part, highly spontaneous and self-directed. Discarnate learning experiences involving master teachers and guides were always unceremonious, informal, individualized, and personally relevant. Our subjects summarized the core curriculum of the afterlife as a combination of pure love and joyful enlightenment—the terms that surfaced over and over in their descriptions of the discarnate realm. These two elements were seen as the primary learning goals and nurturing forces of the cosmos.

Some of our subjects discovered during ascension that they had been discarnate teachers. According to their reports, the major attribute of a discarnate teacher is pure love and the ability express it. The discarnate learning format was always flexible and open-ended, and the learning environment, rather than a self-contained classroom, was anywhere in the cosmos.

Not surprisingly, the accumulated past-life histories of our subjects revealed the indestructible nature of personal consciousness. Although a vast range of themes, patterns, and experiences characterizes our individual evolution, the unifying element in our existence is our uniqueness as an immortal entity. Each past lifetime, and each discarnate interval, come together in a one-of-a-kind cosmic patchwork held together by the powerful thread of evolving personal consciousness.

Past-Life Excursion

For people who are resistant to hypnotic suggestion, but who are, nonetheless, responsive to out-of-body travel, we developed a past-life strategy that relies solely on the out-of-body state. Like Past-life Ascent, this procedure, *Past-Life Excursion*, recognizes the significance of our past-life history, including our pre-incarnate, incarnate, and discarnate past. But rather than accessing higher cosmic archives or scanning our total past-life history, Past-Life Excursion is designed to retrieve only those specific past experiences that are presently relevant to our growth. It recognizes the inner wisdom and power of consciousness, as the storehouse of all our past, to "zero in" on pertinent but hidden experiences, access them, and bring them into conscious awareness. It emphasizes the capacity of consciousness to reprocess selected past experiences and relate them to present growth needs.

Although Past-Life Excursion typically focuses on experiences from past lifetimes only, it can probe the intervals between them, and occasionally it will reach as far back as our earliest pre-incarnate existence. Under the watchful eyes of our higher consciousness and astral guides, only those potentially empowering experiences that we can presently accommodate and process are retrieved. While hypnotic age regression has been known to prematurely release painful experiences from the past, with potentially disempowering consequences, Past-Life Excursion involves a spontaneous but ingenuous selection process that gauges our learning readiness and filters out presently irrelevant or potentially damaging past-life experiences accordingly. When past-life consciousness is raised, our adapting capacity, along with our learning readiness, is likewise raised. Given repeated excursions over time, we become empowered to access and awaken our dormant resources, accelerate our evolution, and eventually, to accommodate even our most painful and threatening past-life experiences.

While recognizing the power of consciousness to probe itself and tap into its own resources, Past-Life Excursion emphasizes the critical importance of higher plane luminaries who willingly accompany the excursion and provide the essential support system for our journey into the past. With the assistance and protection of skilled teachers and guides, we become doubly empowered to access our past and activate our dormant growth potentials.

Past-Life Excursion is a flexible procedure with a single objective: to retrieve and process those past-life experiences—*pre-incarnate, incarnate*, and *discarnate*—that are relevant and potentially empowering to our present growth. But rather than focusing on a quick fix to a present issue or problem, the procedure emphasizes growth and learning. It relies on the wisdom of consciousness, with the assistance of highly evolved astral beings, to manage the excursion experience and guide the learning process associated with it.

Past-Life Excursion is based on two essential principles of growth: the *principle of continuity* and the *principle of cumulative effects*. The principle of continuity holds that our growth is a never-ending process. Whether rapid or slow, smooth or erratic, it is always continuous. It reaches from our earliest pre-incarnate origins to our present existence, and beyond into infinity.

The principle of cumulative effects complements the principle of continuity by asserting that we are, at any given moment, the totality of all our previous experiences, which can span many past lifetimes and the discarnate intervals between them. According to this principle, many of our past experiences are laden with unrealized growth potential. Furthermore, each new learning experience expands our capacity for future growth. Consequently, personal potential, rather than a fixed product, becomes a fluid process of constant change and unfoldment.

Past-Life Excursion stays with the growth continuum by following it into the far-distant past to bring forth enlightenment and heightened awareness of experiences that remain rich in growth potential. Once our past experiences are uncovered, we can identify their empowering potential and activate them to enrich our lives and accelerate our development. In all probability, we will never fully exhaust the wealth of empowering resources available to us from our past.

Past-Life Excursion recognizes the long-term consequences not only of our positive past but also our negative past, including experiences in which we were victims or, even worse, perpetrators of injustice. The procedure equips us to access our past negative experiences, glean insight from them, and break the cycle of disempowerment they often generate. Through *excursion insight*, we not only discover our mistakes, flaws, and vulnerabilities; we also find ways of overcoming them.

In addition to its capacity to retrieve past-life experiences, Past-Life Excursion often stimulates our psychic faculties to access information from other sources. For instance, our awareness of a particular past-life event during Past-Life Excursion is often accompanied by totally new clairvoyant insight concerning the conditions surrounding the event. The result can be a more complete explanation for an otherwise puzzling past-life experience, such as an early death or another unexplained tragedy. Many of the unsolved mysteries of our past can be solved through a combination of Past-Life Excursion and expanded psychic awareness of the past—an ESP phenomenon known as *retrocognition*.

Like two streams that merge, Past-Life Excursion and psychic insight can form a forceful current, teeming with new learning and growth possibilities. This was illustrated by a teacher whose fear of death was so intense that it was a constant source of distress—yet he experienced no ambivalence concerning life after death. He confessed, "I fear death, but not life after it." During excursion, he regressed into his most recent past lifetime and clairvoyantly viewed a servant secretly adding poison to the wine he was later to drink at a banquet. His resulting death was slow and agonizing. His subsequent excursions into other past lifetimes revealed death experiences that were painless and peaceful. He concluded that his fear of death was simply a generalization of the pain and dark mystery surrounding his last death experience. This series of excursions changed his outlook on life and empowered him to resolve his fear of death.

Past-Life Excursion can be profoundly empowering independent of the past-life experiences uncovered by the procedure. Excursioners almost always report a strong bond with the ministering guides who give guidance during the experience. Perhaps even more rewarding is the heightened awareness of a magnificent cosmic life force that almost always accompanies the excursion experience.

A dark (or semi-dark) setting and a comfortable, reclining position are recommended for Past-Life Excursion; it requires approximately one hour during which there must be no interruptions. Here is the procedure:

Step 1. Invocation. The purpose of this step is to call forth the empowering presence of ministering guides. The simple affirmation, *I am empowered by the presence of ministering guides throughout this experience*, is usually sufficient to assure higher plane protection and guidance for the duration the procedure.

Step 2. Out-of-Body Induction. Out-of-body induction for this procedure begins by generating a focused mental state through imagery of a surrounding space filled with light, but devoid of color, shapes, or movement. A strategy called *astral polarization* is then used to induce the out-of-body state. Polarization is initiated by a physical and mental clearing exercise that sets the stage for the out-of-body state. Imagery of the physical body as a sponge soaking in relaxation is recommended for physical clearing, while envisioning the astral body as a tranquil energy form, filled with light, is recommended for mental clearing.

As relaxation and tranquillity deepen, the physical body becomes progressively heavy with relaxation, while the astral body becomes increasingly buoyant with tranquillity. The result is the polarization of the astral and biological bodies, and a slow separation of the two. Allow adequate time for the polarization and separation process to be completed, and for awareness of the out-of-body state to fully emerge.

Step 3. Out-of-Body Excursion. With astral/biological polarization and disengagement now complete, you are ready to initiate out-of-body excursion. The procedure begins by recognizing the presence of ministering guides, followed by spontaneously scanning your existence, from your earliest pre-incarnate beginnings to the present. Envision the scope of your existence as your personal cosmos, a sort of miniature universe. As you view that universe, notice its extensive structure of celestial bodies. Notice the scattered orbs of light, connected by a continuous line of light, against a background of cosmic space. Let your psychic faculties contribute to the spontaneous unfolding of your unique personal cosmos.

The orbs and their connecting lines are highly significant components of your personal cosmos. Each orb of light represents a past life, and each connecting segment of light between the orbs represents a discarnate interval between lives. The arrangement in spatial distance of the orbs and lines represents the chronological order of your past lives and the intervals between them, with the most distant orb representing your first incarnation, and nearest orb representing your most recent incarnation. The orbs and their connecting lines reflect the continuity and permanence of your existence as a conscious, evolving entity. The line of light reaching beyond the most distant orb and stretching into infinity represents your pre-incarnate existence in the universe. Together, these elements and their arrangement form a complete cosmic map of your voyage through time.

Certain characteristics of your cosmic orbs and their connecting lines are critical, because they provide important guidelines for understanding your personal cosmos. The current relevance of each orb or line is gauged by its brightness; the brighter the line or orb, the greater its significance and current growth potential. The size of the orbs and the length of the lines connecting them are measurements of time; the larger the orb, the greater the span of incarnation, and the longer the line, the greater the discarnate interval. On average, long lifetimes are followed by long after-life intervals—typically the result of more discarnate time being required to exhaust the growth resources accumulated over a long lifetime. It would follow that a long lifetime characterized by worthy endeavors would gather abundant growth resources that would require an exceptionally long after-life interval. Quantity, as measured by time, however, does not always signify quality. Occasionally, a very small orb will appear intensely brilliant, an indication that a relative brief lifetime was profoundly significant and continues to possess important growth resources. Likewise, a short but bright line between two orbs reflects a very brief but highly significant growth interval between lifetimes. The brightness of your orbs and lines also reflects your present readiness to accommodate their inventory of resources, with the brighter the points or lines, the greater your readiness to probe them and access their growth potentials.

As you view your cosmic map, you will probably note that bright orbs are usually followed by bright lines. This pattern suggests that significant growth during a given lifetime is typically followed by significant growth in the discarnate interval after that lifetime.

The shape of the lines, aside from their brightness and length, also signifies certain important discarnate growth patterns. Lines that are smooth and straight indicate harmony and security, whereas lines that are rugged and jagged suggest upheaval and turbulence. Lines that turn sharply or climb rapidly reflect important changes in developmental direction, or a crucial testing of endurance. These irregular patterns typically follow several sheltered lifetimes of smooth, even development. But rather than slowing or disrupting our progress, these irregularities actually accelerate our growth. They focus on our specific developmental needs and flex our adaptive muscles. Equally as important, they increase our tolerance for change and empower us to cope with adversity.

As you scan the universe of your past, your attention will probably be drawn first to intensely bright orbs and lines, even though they may appear far away in cosmic life-space. By simply viewing your personal universe and scanning it from a distance, you can spontaneously activate the force fields of particular points and lines. You can then consciously interact with your personal universe. Accompanied by your ministering guides, you will find yourself drawn to the point or line that is relevant for you at the moment. Upon merging with it, you will experience the empowering value of that point or segment of your past. Typically, the past experience unfolds as a detailed projection or a re-enactment, with the degree of your involvement in the experience determined by your own choice and the discretion of your ministering guides.

Step 4. Conclusion. To initiate the out-of-body return, shift your attention away from the excursion experience to your physical body and its surroundings. The affirmation, *I am now ready to end excursion and re-engage my physical body,* is usually sufficient to activate a smooth biological/astral re-engagement. Occasionally, the return will be initiated by a ministering entity, who guides attention away from the excursion experience and into the present. Excursion is concluded by reviewing the experience and further exploring its relevance.

Past-Life Excursion can encompass a complete past lifetime, surveying it from its beginning to its end, or it can selectively examine only a critical fragment of a particularly relevant past life. It can study a life between lives, either in part or in full. Out-of-body excursion often re-engages a past after-life interaction to result in a wondrous renewal of the spirit, or a totally new flash of empowering insight. Previously unheeded experiences can be uncovered and their empowering potential activated.

Repeated past-life excursions can gradually compile a complete record of our personal past-life history. Past lifetimes, and the lives between them, can generate a cosmic map that remains fixed from excursion to excursion. Like the astronomer's map of the stars, our personal cosmic map charts the orbs and lines of our past, and provides an invaluable guide in our quest for enlightenment. While the empowerment potential of our past experiences may never be fully realized, each past-life excursion provides new understanding of our past, while suggesting new possibilities for our future. Of equal importance, each excursion uncovers new empowering resources that can be used to accelerate our growth and enrich our lives in the here and now.

The cosmic map for each person is a stable representation that is uniquely different from the map of any other person. Among the factors that seem to influence the differences among maps are the characteristics of the person. Since our personal evolution encompasses many lifetimes and, of course, the intervals between them, it should not be surprising to find that our personal characteristics are often reflected in our cosmic maps. For instance, cosmic maps with numerous orbs and short connecting lines of only moderate brightness typically characterize the adventurous individual who may be somewhat immature and irresponsible. The brief, dull discarnate intervals characteristic of this pattern suggest a deficiency in accumulated growth resources from past lifetimes and slow discarnate development between lives.

College undergraduates who were asked to draw their personal cosmic maps following their past-life excursions typically drew longer connecting lines between recent points of light, a finding which suggests that a longer period of after-life development may now be required to exhaust the rich resources gathered in contemporary lifetimes. On the other hand, this trend could also suggest poor growth in contemporary lifetimes, so that the learning possibilities are greater today on the other side than on this side. This capacity of discarnate teachers and other growth specialists to make up for a deficiency in our collected resources is called *discarnate compensation*.

In a laboratory project designed to explore inner awareness of personal past-life history, a group of college students were instructed to use *automatic drawing* to depict their past-life cosmic maps prior to out-of-body excursion. The subjects were instructed to clear their minds, and while resting a writing pen on a blank sheet of paper, to allow automatic drawings of personal past-life histories to unfold spontaneously, with circles representing their past lifetimes, and lines representing the discarnate intervals between lifetimes. They then engaged in past-life excursion, after which they drew their cosmic maps as experienced during the excursion.

Comparisons of the two maps revealed amazing similarities. Although it could be argued that the individual's automatic drawing prior to excursion could have influenced the excursion experience and the later drawing, all the subjects in the study interpreted the similarities in their drawings as tangible evidence of a cosmic history permanently inscribed in their personal consciousness as well as in outer cosmic realms.

Along another line, the present career interests and characteristics of our subjects were often suggested in their cosmic map patterns. For instance, a comparison of the maps of engineers and artists drawn after their excursion experiences revealed marked differences. The engineers' were typically linear and characterized by equally spaced orbs of light while the artists' were characterized by greater variation, not only in space between orbs but also in the arrangement of the orbs themselves. This finding suggests that certain past-life patterns could either qualify or predispose us to pursue certain careers. Given further research, the personal cosmic map could become a valuable tool for identifying career interests and guiding career choices.

As already noted, cosmic maps are characterized by a pre-incarnate line reaching backward from the most distant incarnate orb and extending into infinity. Excursion subjects who focused their repeated excursion efforts on that segment of their cosmic maps were highly consistent in their descriptions of pre-incarnate life. The pre-incarnate state of awareness was described as *expansive consciousness*—a term that was used by almost all the excursioners. In that state, personal identity was intact and there was acute awareness of being a unique, independent entity.

Typically, excursioners experience the pre-incarnate reality as a magnificent dimension filled with brightness and beauty. They often compare it to a magical, moonlit landscape with fluid-like forms and luminous planes. Radiant colors that span the spectrum are prominent in their descriptions. Interestingly, excursioners describe themselves and others as imperfect, yet possessing unlimited growth potential. Flaws and weaknesses in pre-incarnate (and other stages of) development are seen as growth challenges, not irreversible defects.

Out-of-body excursioners frequently discover a strong affinity with those they have encountered during their pre-incarnate probes—such interactions are invariably spontaneous and rewarding. Special relationships are often uncovered, and some excursioners find that their present soulmate relationships originated in their pre-incarnate past.

The following descriptions of pre-incarnate life were taken from the excursion summaries of college students who used a series of Past-Life Excursions to probe their pre-incarnate existence:

- I was an independent entity who was totally aware of my own being as well as the presence of others.

- I knew that I was among friends, some of whom, in retrospect, I recognize as my friends today.

- In the pre-incarnate state, I was without inhibitions. Sharing was easy. I experienced oneness with every aspect of the pre-incarnate dimension.

- I knew no limitations; time and space were irrelevant.

- I was complete in myself and an integral part of cosmos.

- My pre-incarnate existence was a part of a greater presence, and my being was a part of a greater being. I was in touch with the universe.

- ◆ Brightness and freedom were everywhere.

- ◆ Communication was spontaneous and easy.

- ◆ I recognized certain entities as highly evolved, but equality and oneness rather than rank prevailed.

- ◆ Love, security, and compassion were everywhere. It was a heavenly place.

Following their pre-incarnate probes, excursioners almost always experience a deeper understanding of themselves and their origins. They discover new meaning to their lives, and a new sense of their oneness with the cosmos. Enlightened and renewed by the experience, they see life from a refreshing new perspective that spans the totality of their existence—past, present and future.

Although pre-incarnate excursion is, in reality, a return to one's deepest past, it is often experienced by excursioners as a current reality rather than as a probe of pre-incarnate existence. Even upon returning to the body and reminding themselves that the experience was a journey into their past, they often remain somewhat uncertain about the "past versus present" nature of the experience. With repeated excursions, however, most subjects become increasingly convinced that their excursions are accurately probing their pre-incarnate past. It is conceivable, nevertheless, that an experience that we label a pre-incarnate excursion could also include out-of-body travel to a present astral plane.

The travel reports of excursioners also reveal marked similarities between the pre-incarnate and the discarnate dimensions. In both, personal growth is experienced as continuously evolving. Excursioners travelling in both dimensions consistently experienced an unwavering sense of personal worth and infinite identity during the experience. The astral body image, like the identity, also remains unchanged from excursion to excursion. Excursioners are consistent in their beliefs that the astral body consists of cosmic matter arranged in ways that provide the astral genesis of identity. Incarnation is seen simply as the embodiment of cosmic identity in a biological structure. Conversely, the out-of-body state is seen as the temporary astral liberation of cosmic identity from the biological body.

Excursioners often discover that they have had meaningful past experiences with animals during their pre-incarnate and discarnate existences.

As they explore their past-life history, excursioners invariably develop a deeper respect for animals, and a stronger recognition of their rights as creatures of dignity and worth. For many of excursioners, this is one of the major benefits of the excursion experience. Many excursioners discover a familiar soulmate animal who, like a special friend, has been their companion from life to life.

Excursioners often discover advanced teachers, guides, and ministering angels in their pre-incarnate and discarnate past. Many of these astral luminaries appear again and again in the afterlife realm, and excursioners often find that a particular luminary had become their permanent, lifelong guide. Many excursioners report "re-experiencing" many of their past *astral group sessions* in which they interacted with astral luminaries and were enlightened concerning the nature of the spiritual cosmos and their personal evolution.

Experienced excursioners are unanimous in the belief that the after-life dimension is stable in both element and form. They conclude that the cosmic principles of the afterlife are basic to our understanding of the physical composition and properties of the universe. They note, however, that the discarnate realm is not ruled by the principles of physics as we know them. In that dimension, conventional concepts of time, space, and material form are superseded by a liberated awareness of the intangible or spiritual substance underlying all tangible realities. Tangible reality, according to excursioners, is a creation of the intangible; its existence is simply a material manifestation of the spiritual. Excursioners found that physical reality and physical existence simply provide temporary conditions to support our spiritual evolution. Once our spiritual evolution is complete, there is no pressing need for additional lifetimes in the physical realm—with the possible exception of additional lifetimes devoted to helping others in their personal evolution. It would logically follow, that once spiritual evolution on a global scale is realized, the life-support system we call the physical realm will become irrelevant.

Excursioners agree that the cosmic life force is the energizing foundation of all reality, both tangible and intangible. The miracle of our immortality, and the flawless design of the universe, are manifestations of that force in its highest and noblest form. In the absence of that creative cosmic force, intangible as well as tangible reality would cease to exist.

Taken together, the results of past-life excursion consistently confirm the cumulative nature of our past growth and the permanence of conscious identity. According to the ministering guide of one past-life excursioner, "Each past, present, and future lifetime is a priceless pearl on the endless string of cosmic consciousness."

The superior effectiveness of OBEs in exploring our individual past-life history is due largely to the transcendent nature of the out-of-body state and our capacity to use it as a past-life enlightenment strategy. Advanced out-of-body strategies, such as Past-Life Excursion and Past-Life Ascent, can lift personal consciousness to new levels, awaken dormant inner potential, and create new growth options. Many of the mysteries we encounter in life can undoubtedly be solved by exploring our past lives and the discarnate intervals between them. Past-life enlightenment reveals the richness of our past, the purposefulness of our present, and the exciting possibilities that await each of us.

9

OBEs and Higher Planes

The unexamined life is not worth living.

Socrates, in Plato's *Apology*

O UR PHYSICAL ENVIRONMENT as we know it is only one of many dimensions within a larger multi-dimensional system. Within that system is a dimension we call the spiritual. Tangible reality, including our biological existence in the physical universe, is a material manifestation of a higher, spiritual reality. Because we are in essence spiritual beings in both origin and destiny, it should not be surprising that we can access and interact with the spiritual domain, of which we are an integral part.

The empowering dynamics of the spiritual dimension involve two essential elements: 1) the intrinsically empowering design of that dimension and its multiple planes, and 2) the wealth of enlightening resources found within them, including teachers, guides, angels, and advanced discarnates. By simply tapping into higher planes, we can draw on their limitless potential to enlighten, inspire, and heal the mind, body, and spirit—resulting in an instant surge of growth and power. By personally interacting with higher plane entities, we can further enrich our lives with even greater power and new growth possibilities. To overlook the power potential of the higher planes is to dismiss the most critical source of personal empowerment available to us.

The out-of-body experience remains the primary instrument through which we can *literally* ascend to distant spiritual realities and directly interact with them. OBEs make up the centerpiece of an evolving technology that liberates us to experience our spiritual being and travel out-of-body to directly access the rich resources of the higher astral planes. This supremely challenging application of OBEs opens the door to exciting new discoveries about ourselves and our existence, as well as the nature of the astral realm.

The astral dimension, while often considered distant and mysterious, is in some ways similar to the astral body itself. Both are spiritual counterparts of the physical, and both transcend the laws of physics that rule the physical universe. Of equal, if not greater importance, is the fact that both are permanent, indestructible forces in the cosmos. Because we are, in essence, spiritual beings, we are by nature connected to the larger cosmos, whose essence is also spiritual. When we enter the out-of-body state, we spontaneously engage the astral dimension, where we have ready access to higher astral planes. Through the out-of-body experience, we can become active participants in an exciting, interactive process of growth and discovery.

Although spontaneous OBEs often engage higher astral planes, several procedures have been specifically structured to generate astral probes and interactions. Some of these strategies are designed simply to introduce us to higher astral planes, whereas others are structured to promote an energizing interaction with them. While these procedures differ, in both design and conceptualization, they share a common goal: personal empowerment and enlightenment.

Among the most advanced out-of-body procedures are those specifically formulated to initiate out-of-body interactions with highly specialized astral teachers and guides. These procedures can target a particular growth need, or they can focus on a wide range of practical issues, such as financial success, relationships, health needs, rejuvenation—or even sensuous pleasure. These applications, while essentially temporal, are important because they help us fulfill certain basic needs indirectly related to our spiritual evolution. It should be emphasized, however, that our interactions with the astral domain must eventually rise above temporal concerns and focus directly on our higher spiritual needs.

The higher planes offer an array of growth resources that can meet an extensive range of developmental needs. Fortunately, in the astral realm, diversity and flexibility outweigh conformity and structure. Nevertheless, those with a strong need for structure in their lives often discover highly structured astral planes; while those who value autonomy almost invariably experience astral planes in which they find complete freedom. Similarly, those with highly conservative values often find a corresponding astral plane; while individuals with highly liberal values tend to experience astral interactions that validate their value system. These features of astral planes, rather than diminishing the value of OBEs, reveal the nurturing nature of the astral dimension, and its capacity to adapt to our development level and our comfort needs. With repeated travel, however, we tend to progressively evolve toward more mature, enlightening astral interactions.

In many ways, the astral dimension is like the university system of higher education, with the various levels of astral planes comparable to the various levels of the university curriculum. Like the university system, the astral dimension is both flexible and diverse. Discarnates, like university students, progress at their own pace from level to level in their pursuit of knowledge. They specialize in certain major areas, and pursue a variety of elective enrichment experiences. Occasionally, they transfer to totally new programs or specialty areas. Like university students, discarnates share many common experiences designed to equip them with basic skills and essential knowledge. And like the university system, the discarnate realm utilizes skilled specialists to guide learning and development. Like the university library, an archival system housing complete cosmic records is maintained in the discarnate realm. Finally, like the university system—whose resources are typically available to its students and to the wider community alike—the abundant resources of the astral dimension are offered, not only to discarnates, but to each of us through our out-of-body visits and interactions.

Our analysis of the OBEs of hundreds of subjects consistently revealed the positive nature of their higher-plane interactions. Our subjects, who were characteristically accompanied in their OBEs by ministering guides, reported no negative encounters in their out-of-body travels to higher astral planes. Such highly positive results could be attributed to OBEs procedures that emphasized the accompaniment of ministering guides throughout the out-of-body experience. Our subjects concluded that the threats occasionally reported by out-of-body explorers are most probably of inner origin—or else, the result of inadequate preparation, or faulty out-of-body procedures.

According to our subjects, there is no plausible reason or need for negativity in the higher astral realm. Their interactions with advanced entities consistently revealed that the negative forces found in our temporal reality have no functional role or purpose in the astral realm. Our subjects concluded that the struggles and hurting conflicts experienced by many discarnates, rather than originating in the astral realm, result from negative experiences or karmic baggage carried over from past life. To quote one discarnate teacher, "Negative effects are counterpoised and absolved only by positive effects." We could conclude that the disproportionate negativity generated at the temporal level demands positive intervention at the astral level. Wherever we are in our personal evolution, we can each contribute to that intervention effort by generating positive energy and sending it forth into the universe.

Our subjects found the structure of discarnate reality to be orderly, but far less rigid than they had earlier conceived. Rather than a clearly defined power hierarchy among astral planes or the entities within them, they discovered continuity and harmony, with each plane contributing to the larger evolving cosmic spiral. The concept of "higher versus lower" astral planes seemed relevant only to certain evolutionary features within the greater cosmic spiral, rather than to the plane's status or prestige.

Out-of-body explorers typically describe the astral domain as a safe place of *peace, love,* and *joy.* They were characteristically autonomous and free of restrictions in their probes of astral realities. All planes were available to astral travelers and their ministering guides. Astral specialists or facilitators, who exist in all cosmic planes—and appear, in fact, to move freely among them—were present to guide out-of-body travels and accompany them from plane to plane. No resources within planes were withheld from the out-of-body explorer. Invariably, astral travelers viewed their out-of-body interactions with astral planes as a preview of their own discarnate future.

The evidence gleaned from out-of-body accounts suggests that the astral planes, while similar to each other in many ways, differ significantly in their particular specialties and purposes. The wide-ranging specialties found among planes included adaptation, wholeness, enlightenment, discovery, learning, loving, and play—to list but a few. Interestingly, one out-of-body traveler, who was incidentally known for his great sense of humor, discovered a unique plane he called *joyful laughter*, which he believed to be among the most powerful planes in the cosmos.

In the astral domain, discarnates—along with astral specialists such as angels, guides, facilitators, and teachers—seem to share a common commitment: *continuous growth* and *spiritual actualization*. That commitment, astral travelers agree, is equally applicable to life on our planet. At a personal level, it leads to action and creative living. On a broader scale, it lifts global consciousness and makes the planet a better place for ourselves and future incarnates.

The discarnate state is the personification of our highest and best possibilities. Out-of-body travelers typically describe discarnates as engaging, energetic beings who have assumed a wondrous intangible form while retaining easily recognizable but brightly transformed features. Through discarnate transformation, they reclaim at once the prime of their past lives and the peaks of their past achievements. They continue to pursue their dreams and highest hopes. Physical imperfections, including those associated with heredity, deprivation, injury, aging, and illness, take on a spiritual character and a flawless beauty.

Every out-of-body interaction with the spiritual dimension is potentially empowering. Even highly passive probes in which we simply view the higher astral planes from a distance can energize and stimulate new growth. But by interfacing and interacting with them, we can draw more abundantly from their powerful resources. At a deep personal level, we can interact with astral specialists, such as advanced discarnates and teachers, who willingly help us to discover our individual growth needs and ways of fulfilling them. Many out-of-body travelers experience deeply meaningful interactions with departed loved ones. Important issues, such as grief, guilt, and fear, can be almost instantly resolved through astral interactions in the caring presence of benevolent guides.

As in past-life excursions, out-of-body interactions involving higher astral planes often reveal the presence of animals on the other side. In one instance, a student was joyfully reunited with the horse that had been his companion throughout his childhood. Upon meeting, they immediately recognized each other. Riding bareback over cosmic terrain, he experienced anew his enduring love for the animal, who had been a childhood friend he would never forget. He noted, "The other side would be incomplete without animals." All of us who have lost an animal friend can relate to his experience. When death comes to our cherished animals, it is comforting to know that they, too, will cross over to the other side. Among the major indices of our personal evolution is respect for animals and a recognition of their dignity and worth. Our own future transition will be enriched by a beautiful reunion with significant others, including our departed animals.

Out-of-body accounts, while revealing strong similarities between the various astral planes, also indicate marked differences in their design and configuration. Always exquisitely structured, astral planes often appear as bright, three-dimensional regions, with wide variations in expansiveness, luminosity, and coloration. Certain planes appear as almost concrete realities, with such features as colorful gardens, pools, expansive terrain, and even sculpted structures. Other planes appear in magical forms of smooth, flowing, and colorful energy. The fact that some planes are situated above other planes, however, does not suggest a hierarchy of power or influence.

In the discarnate realm, planes are seen primarily as energized growth environments. Each plane focuses its particular empowerment resources and growth facilitators on meeting the growth needs of discarnates. Rather than being locked into a specific plane, discarnates, like out-of-body travelers, move freely among planes, depending on their preferences and growth needs. Ascending within planes and among them simply signifies progress toward enlightenment and spiritual actualization—the ultimate goal of our existence in the cosmos.

According to astral travelers, colors of all the hues of the spectrum—including wave frequencies outside the range of normal human perception—characterize the astral dimension. Certain planes are multicolored, whereas others appear in shades of a particular color, such as violet, blue, yellow, orange, or green. These planes of color appear to be energized by an enormous central dimension of pure white light. Black astral planes, and black spaces among planes, do not exist in the higher astral realm.

OBEs involving higher astral planes, including interactions with advanced astral entities, consistently reveal the significance of astral coloration as an index of the growth specialty of a particular astral plane. Multi-colored planes, which are among the most common, typically focus on cosmic rudiments and comprehensive developmental needs. They are usually vast in size and vibrating with activity. They provide a myriad of growth and learning experiences designed to empower their participants to overcome their growth barriers and unleash their inner potential.

In contrast to the multi-colored planes, each astral plane of a given color focuses on a more specific goal. Violet planes, which are extremely responsive to OBEs, facilitate spiritual actualization, while yellow planes are known to stimulate learning and cognitive development. Blue planes, which are very numerous, promote balance and cosmic harmony. Green planes are valued for their healing powers. Orange planes specialize in motivation and nurturance. Red planes, which are rare, are associated with sharp cosmic intervention and redirection.

It is interesting to note that the empowering effects of higher plane interactions can typically be seen in the aura after the out-of-body experience. The human aura, the energy field surrounding the physical body, is often considered to be the external manifestation of the inner life force. It is seen by some to represent the essence of our existence as an enduring energy system in the universe. Following out-of-body interactions with multi-colored astral planes, the aura becomes more expansive, and takes on an array of colors with new clarity and brilliance. Interacting with a plane of a specific color energizes the aura with that color and the benefits associated with it. For instance, the green plane energizes the aura with bright green, and empowers our energy system with the rejuvenation and health benefits associated with that plane; whereas interaction with the yellow plane energizes the aura with that color while increasing intellectual skills, improving memory, and accelerating the rate of learning. The yellow plane is very popular among college students skilled in out-of-body travel.

With even limited practice, almost anyone will experience the empowering effects of the multi-colored planes, as well as the other empowering benefits associated with planes of other colors. OBEs involving more highly specialized planes, however, typically follow at least some experience with the multi-colored planes.

Astral Outsourcing

One of the most effective strategies for accessing and interacting with higher planes is *Astral Outsourcing*. This interactive approach is a very practical, sensible procedure for exploring a highly relevant yet rarely experienced dimension of reality. Astral Outsourcing involves a single objective: the acquisition of new growth resources through out-of-body interactions with higher planes. Through this procedure, we can actively engage various astral planes and interact with evolving discarnates, as well as advanced astral entities, including angels, guides, teachers, and other specialized growth facilitators. Although the term itself may sound mechanical, growth facilitators are, in reality, loving, caring, and benevolent beings whose primary role is to offer loving support and inspire our full evolution.

The astral planes are readily available to all out-sourcing travelers who wish to enter them. Growth facilitators, who exist in all cosmic planes, move freely among planes and are always present to escort out-of-body travelers from plane to plane. No plane is off-limits, and no resource within planes is withheld from our out-sourcing probes. Astral Outsourcing is structured to initiate astral travel and gather the astral resources relevant to our present growth. Here is the procedure:

Step 1. Outsourcing Preliminaries. Approximately one hour should be allowed for Astral Outsourcing, during which there must be no distractions. The procedure is best done in a reclining position, with the legs uncrossed and the arms resting comfortably at the sides. To begin the procedure, specify your goals, then relax your physical body with the use of cognitive techniques such as body scan, deep breathing, and peaceful mental imagery. Once your body is fully relaxed, begin repeating positive affirmations to facilitate travel and empowering interactions. For this procedure, saying the affirmations out loud seems to make them more effective. Examples of recommended affirmations are:

I am surrounded by peace and tranquillity as I travel out-of-body to experience the highest realms of spiritual reality. I am sheltered and protected by caring guides who are my constant companions throughout this experience. The limitless wisdom and power of the cosmos await my search and welcome my interaction.

Step 2. Outsourcing Induction. To induce the out-of-body state, close your eyes and envision your physical body at rest. Take as much time as you need to form a clear image of your physical body, then envision your astral double as a light form bearing consciousness, rising gently upward and away. Once you reach a full sense of separation from your physical body, mentally re-affirm your intent to explore distant astral realms and engage the presence of accompanying astral guides. Use imagery of distant planes and astral guides to reinforce your affirmations. At this point in the procedure, you will likely experience the unmistakable presence of astral guides, as they ascend with you toward the spiritual planes. Upon reaching the spiritual dimension, many travelers experience wonder at the breaking of the cosmic energy barrier and the awesome emergence of the astral realm. Entrance into that splendid realm is almost always accompanied by awareness of multiple colors and a magnificent infusion of cosmic energy, along with a sense of belonging and oneness with the universe.

Step 3. Multi-colored Outsourcing. At this step, the infusion of cosmic energy continues, as you engage the multi-colored astral plane. If you have practiced *Past-Life Excursion,* or other regression procedures that explore life between lives, you will immediately recognize this familiar zone, in which teachers, guides, angels, and other ministering entities appear as warm, nurturing friends rather than cold, distant authorities. Telepathy is the common communication mode, and pure love characterizes every empowering interaction. Discarnates, some of whom are familiar, are typically present in indescribably beautiful surroundings.

The major resource of the multi-colored plane is cosmic love, the essential element in our spiritual evolution. You can infuse yourself with pure cosmic love simply by lingering in this dimension and interacting with its growth facilitators. Cosmic love is the most powerful force in the universe. It empowers our entire being—mentally, physically, and spiritually—with positive energy and vitality. A full infusion of cosmic love provides the basic foundation for outsourcing the more highly specialized planes in the cosmos.

Although deeply personal interactions with discarnates can occur while outsourcing other planes, they often unfold at this level. Common examples are joyful reunions with the departed, including relatives, friends, and animals. These interactions are invariably empowering for all involved.

Step 4. Specialized Outsourcing. At this point, you can choose to conclude the outsourcing experience, and go directly to Step 5, or you can continue by tapping into the more specific resources of the other planes with *Specialized Outsourcing*. Numerous specialized planes, each characterized by a different color that signifies its empowerment specialty, are available for outsourcing.

The specialized planes most frequently experienced during outsourcing are violet, blue, green, yellow, orange, and red. (The pure white energy realm is experienced by astral travelers only indirectly, as a distant source of energy and coloration for all planes.) Each plane has its own resources, growth frequencies, and specialized growth facilitators. Ministering guides pass freely among the various planes, and often escort out-of-body travelers from plane to plane. Visits among different planes can be spontaneous or by personal choice and collaboration with astral guides.

Outsourcing the Violet Plane

The violet astral planes, among the most brilliant in the cosmos, are associated with spiritual enlightenment and actualization. They are usually situated near the brilliant white light at the center of the celestial cosmos. Interactions with violet planes and their growth facilitators are both enlightening and inspiring. They can answer questions concerning the purpose of our lives and the meaning of our existence—past, present, and future. They can connect us to the highest power force in the cosmos. They can balance our lives and bring us into a state of oneness with all that exists. Temporal dilemmas and anxieties all succumb to empowering interactions with this unique plane. Hopelessness and despair are replaced by faith and inner peace.

Typically, the violet planes are vividly evident to the astral traveler. Rather than flat and fixed, they usually appear in a vibrant, orb-like form, without clearly defined borders. The central regions of the plane are intensely violet, whereas the outer edges fade into pale, pastel shades. Violet planes are usually in close proximity to multi-colored planes, with their outer edges often merging, to facilitate easy passage.

To negotiate the violet plane, focus your attention on the plane and affirm your desire to experience its empowering resources. Once affirmed, your desire is spontaneously communicated to ministering guides, who will in turn accompany you, usually hand-in-hand, to that plane.

Upon entering the violet plane, you will find yourself suddenly bathed in a violet radiance. But your attention, rather than remaining focused on surrounding conditions, will invariably shift to the wondrous enlightenment and energizing power that permeates your total being. Once in the violet plane, your empowerment needs are usually known even before your express them. Insight, answers, and solutions spring forth effortlessly. The surge of enlightenment at this stage often lifts our awareness to levels never experienced before. Along with enlightenment, total love—for self and others—tends to flow freely. Outsourcing from this plane will dissolve all hostility, revenge, ill will, and hatred.

Throughout the intricate corridors of the violet plane we find angels, guides, discarnates, and other astral travelers, all bathed in violet radiance. They are all participants and partakers in the powerful inspiration and enlightenment freely flowing throughout this plane. "*Lost in bliss*" is the term often used by astral travelers to describe the unparalleled effect of the violet plane. Understandably, out-of-body visitors to this plane are often reluctant to leave it.

Outsourcing the Blue Plane
Blue planes, numerous in the cosmos, are valued for their balancing and attuning qualities. The blue plane is universally attracting, and many travelers are inexorably drawn to it. You can voluntarily enter the blue plane simply by focusing on the plane and communicating your intent to the ministering guides who are always present as helpers during outsourcing. Travelers who need balance

and harmony in their lives will particularly benefit from interactions with this plane.

Upon entering this plane, we experience an instant, magnificent infusion of peace. Anxiety, insecurity, isolation, and rejection are all replaced by vibrations of harmony and well-being. The stresses of everyday life—problem relationships, job pressures, financial difficulties—suddenly seem manageable, rather than overwhelming.

Accompanied by outsourcing guides, you may choose to negotiate the deep interiors of this plane—where its energies reverberate in a beautiful symphony of power. By lingering in that region of blue light, you will discover the ultimate balancing and attuning effects of this tranquil plane.

Through your interactions with this plane, you can discover the growth side of adversity and your power to release whatever you no longer need. You will find that your weaknesses are easily balanced by your strengths, once you become aware of them. You will discover your ability to give and receive love gladly. Once attuned to your inner feelings and callings, you will experience a wondrous and constant connection to this remarkable plane, and you will probably find yourself visiting it time and time again.

Outsourcing the Green Plane

Astral planes of green are known primarily for their mental, spiritual, and physical healing powers. The astral body, when bathed in the energies of this plane, becomes revitalized and empowered to transport healing energy to the physical body at rest in its distant physical setting. The result can be a powerful infusion of mental, spiritual, and physical rejuvenation.

Illnesses that involve contributing psychological factors are especially responsive to this plane's healing energies. Although more research is needed to evaluate this plane's healing properties, exploratory studies suggest that recovery from even serious psychiatric disorders—such as depression, obsessive-compulsive disorder, and post-traumatic stress disorder—can be accelerated through astral interaction with this plane. Outsourcing this plane has also shown promise in drug treatment programs—alcohol dependency is particularly responsive to outsourcing the green plane.

Outsourcing this plane is often a spontaneous process guided by our health needs. This plane is expansive and highly visible, radiating power and glowing in verdant splendor. Its prominence and attraction command our attention, with the degree of its appeal being the best gauge of our need for its resources. Since we are not always aware of our specific health needs—whether mental, physical, or spiritual—attentiveness to the green plane and responsiveness to its appeal can be critical to our growth and well-being.

To negotiate the green plane, focus your awareness on its gravitation-like force and give yourself permission to be drawn further into its force field. Entry into this plane is usually gradual, with progressive infusions of vitality and rejuvenation. Upon fully engaging this plane, most travelers experience a peak infusion of healing warmth—which can be deliberately transported, by simple intent, to the physical body.

Spiritual renewal almost always accompanies outsourcing this plane. Profound spiritual transformations, with important changes in deep-seated belief systems are not unusual. Refreshing new insights and increased awareness of the spiritual dimension and the presence of ministering angels in daily life often follow a single interaction with this plane. Feelings of worthlessness, inferiority, and despair give way to self-esteem, optimism, faith, and love—all of which are renewed with each visit to this healing plane. Its abundant resources are available to all who enter it—discarnates and outsourcing incarnates alike.

Outsourcing the Yellow Plane

Planes of yellow are important to our personal empowerment because of their capacity to promote learning and intellectual growth. Maximizing the empowering effects of the yellow plane, however, usually requires a series of out-of-body travels that recognize the plane's unique characteristics and our capacity to interact with them. Over time, outsourcing this plane can literally raise our IQ.

The yellow plane often exists in proximity to the green plane, with the frequencies of the two planes merging to form an orange plane between them. The fundamental skills acquired through formal education—such as language, computation, problem solving, and reasoning—are among the specialized resources of this plane.

The learning environment of this plane is flexible but orderly, with many learning facilitators, skilled specialists, and structured learning activities. Instruction, individually and in groups, is always geared to the developmental level of the learner. The instructional goals are clearly defined, and the learning activities are outcome-based. The highly personalized teaching methods emphasize the exchange of knowledge and meaningful interaction, in which every-one—instructor, growth facilitator, resource specialist, and student—participates and learns.

Astral roles in this plane are flexible and adaptable. Students often come forth as facilitators to guide the learning of others, and resource specialists often become students, to learn from other students in an ongoing learning interaction. Diversity, not conformity, is celebrated, and many sources of knowledge are recognized. The cardinal rule of this plane, simply stated, is: *Ultimate truth must arise from within.* The major goal of instruction is to *attune the learner to the master teacher within.*

Outsourcing the Orange Plane

Motivation and nurturance are the specialty of the orange astral planes. Orange planes typically serve as easy passageways or gateways to other planes. Typically situated between yellow and green planes, they combine the frequencies of both to motivate learning and nurture healthful change.

Although few ministering entities or growth facilitators are found in orange planes, interacting with this plane provides excellent preparation for maximizing the benefits of other planes, particularly the enlightening resources offered by the yellow planes and the healing effects of the green planes. Orange planes are often valued for their relaxed atmosphere and comforting effects. Even brief excursions into the orange plane can promote learning-readiness and a general state of well-being. The benefits of outsourcing other specialized planes are spontaneously nurtured through experiencing the energies of the orange plane.

Outsourcing the Red Plane

The red plane is one of the most intensely powerful planes in the cosmos. This plane's primary functions are short-term intervention and fast-paced remediation, under the auspices of highly trained astral specialists. Discarnates who are spiritually underdeveloped, or who carry negative past-life baggage, can be instantly empowered by outsourcing and interacting with this plane. The red plane is also empowering to the inexperienced or somewhat unevolved out-of-body traveler.

Intense and often highly directed strategies, including cognitive re-organization, are among those used by the red plane's advanced teachers and facilitators. Group activities, some of which resemble conventional group therapy, along with one-on-one interactions, characterize many of this plane's activities. Spiritual empowerment and release of negative past-life baggage are emphasized through activities such as *astral reversal* and *cognitive intervention* under the guidance of highly skilled growth facilitators.

Astral reversal is often used as a rectification process, in which we personally experience the adverse effects of our past actions against others. Through astral reversal, we can develop a better understanding of our developmental needs and the consequences of our actions. Perpetrators of violence, for instance, experience the full intensity of the consequences of their acts. Astral reversal, which can be a very lengthy process, is followed by cognitive intervention, in which all negative residue is expiated, and thwarted growth processes are unblocked. In contrast to astral reversal, cognitive intervention directly uncovers disempowering attitudes and self-defeating belief systems, while promoting positive change in cognitive functions.

Out-of-body travelers who enter the red plane usually experience a searching review of their lives, including fleeting glimpses of important past incarnations. Although astral outsourcing with this plane is brief, it can uncover critical growth blockages and identify effective ways of overcoming them.

Following interaction with the red plane, outsourcing the green plane to infuse the mind, body, and spirit with healing energy is recommended.

Step 5. Outsourcing Return and Conclusion. Astral return to the biological body begins with the conscious intent to end outsourcing, followed by the simple affirmation: *I am now ready to return to my physical body*. Attention is then focused on the physical body at rest in its familiar environment, followed by awareness of accompanying guides and a gentle re-entry. Physical sensations will signal the completion of full astral/biological re-engagement.

Astral outsourcing is concluded by a brief period of contemplation, followed by affirmations that highlight the empowering effects of the experience. Examples are:

I am at my peak mentally, physically, and spiritually. I am aware of my potentials, and I am empowered to develop them. I am enveloped in peace and tranquillity. My life is filled with love and joy. I believe in myself and the power within. I am attuned to the highest powers of the cosmos.

These concluding summary statements can be supplemented by globally relevant affirmations, such as:

I am committed to helping others and making the planet a better place. I will use my resources to prevent human and animal and abuse. I will work toward ending hunger and poverty wherever they are found in the world. I will help promote world peace.

Outsourcing Applications

Astral Outsourcing is applicable to a wide range of self-empowerment goals, from promoting wellness to accelerating learning, from rejuvenation to spiritual enlightenment. Outsourcing interactions with the green planes have been effective in alleviating chronic pain and promoting a state of general wellness. An engineer with a history of chronic back pain experienced a marked reduction in pain following a single outsourcing visitation to a green astral plane. In the series of daily visitations that followed, he underwent a procedure he called "green astral massage" in which specialized facilitators gently stroked his astral body to balance and revitalize his energy system. He steadily improved with each visit—and eventually, the pain that had plagued him for many years ended altogether.

The rejuvenating effects of the green planes have been repeatedly demonstrated through astral outsourcing, by both men and women. The visible effects of aging are immediately reduced by outsourcing that seems to collect healthful energy and transfer it to the physical body. The visible wear-and-tear effects of stress on the physical body seem particularly vulnerable to outsourcing this plane. During outsourcing, enlightened astral specialists often focus on specific organ functions or biological systems, energizing and rejuvenating them with healthful vitality.

Negative mental states that can dominate our lives are also sensitive to the energies of the green astral plane. In the therapeutic setting, patients suffering from anxiety or depression rapidly improved when outsourcing this plane was introduced into their treatment programs. Suicidal ideations disappeared altogether, and a marked improvement in mood state was immediately evident.

A favorite outsourcing destination among college students is the yellow plane. Our studies revealed that both memory and learning rates of students enrolled in college-level courses rapidly accelerated when outsourcing the yellow plane was introduced. Mathematics, natural sciences, and languages seemed to be particularly amenable to this strategy. One student, a doctoral candidate with no background in the language, acquired a reading competency in French (one of the requirements for his degree) within six weeks. He attributed his remarkable achievement largely to outsourcing the yellow plane, a strategy he incorporated daily into his study program.

Equally as remarkable as the outsourcing results associated with the green and yellow planes, are the empowering effects of the blue plane. This plane is particularly relevant to life situations involving adversity or personal misfortune. For instance, the stress resulting from a broken relationship, the loss of a job, or the death of a family member or friend can disrupt our lives and deplete our coping resources. Under these conditions, outsourcing the blue plane can restore balance to our lives and attune us to cosmic sources of unlimited power.

The violet plane is a primary source of spiritual power. When our existence seems meaningless, or without direction, accessing the violet plane can give new hope and purpose to our lives. Persons who outsource this plane often describe the experience as a transformation of the spirit and a rebirth of the inner self. One subject, following his first interaction with this plane, exclaimed, "I will never be the same again." The abiding effect of outsourcing this plane is unconditional love for oneself and others. It is impossible to interact with this plane and not experience a greater love of life and new sense of meaning of one's existence.

In summary, out-of-body interactions with higher astral planes are a celebration of our existence and the abundance of life in the universe. As we travel among astral planes and dimensions, we experience the magnificence of our existence as a permanent force in the universe, and our intimate connection with all that exists in the cosmos. OBEs reveal the wonder of the astral realm with its many planes of varying designs and diverse manifestations. Through OBEs, we can discover that each of us, along with angels, spirit guides, discarnates, and all the other beings in the cosmos share a common goal—to develop our highest potential and to achieve our highest destiny.

10

OBEs in the Laboratory

There is nothing so powerful as truth
—and often nothing so strange.

Daniel Webster

SCIENTISTS, PHILOSOPHERS, THEOLOGIANS, and educators are all participants in the timeless search for new and better ways of understanding
the nature of human existence and the universe. Although their methods
and approaches vary, their goals are essentially the same: to explore the
unknown and expand the borders of knowledge.

Increasingly, researchers from many disciplines are questioning conventional methodologies and established assumptions about human
behavior. They recognize that scientific fact and fiction often collide—as
yesterday's fiction becomes today's science, and today's science becomes
tomorrow's fiction. They also recognize that what we know today is but a
small fraction of what remains unknown.

The scientific study of out-of-body experiences is important for several
reasons. Through controlled investigations, we can explore the nature of the
out-of-body state and uncover its underlying dynamics. We can identify the
variables associated with successful OBEs, and discover the relationships
between OBEs and other altered states. Through research, we can develop
the strategies required for inducing the out-of-body state and directing it

toward specific empowerment goals. Finally, scientific research can replace speculation with fact, and provide the foundation for further study.

The studies that follow were designed to explore the out-of-body state and penetrate the shroud of mystery that all too often clouds our understanding of this potentially empowering phenomenon.

OBEs and Electrophotography

Efforts to photograph the astral body in its projected form have been only marginally successful. Using advanced photographic procedures, the projected astral body has been recorded, under certain conditions, either as a point or as a small bar of light, which is believed by some investigators to be the astral body's energizing core. Only rarely will an expansive light form appear in the photograph. Similarly, efforts to photograph discarnate beings, as during a seance or table-tilting, typically record only points of light or minute bars of bright energy.

Fortunately, efforts to photograph *electromagnetic energy patterns* around the physical body during OBEs have met with greater success. Using *electrophotography*—also known as *Kirlian photography* or *corona-discharge photography*—our laboratory research revealed marked changes in the electromagnetic energy patterns surrounding the physical body during the out-of-body state. For this research, we devised an experimental situation in which the energy patterns surrounding the right index finger could be monitored during OBEs, as the physical body remained at rest on a couch.

Developed by the Russian scientists Semyon and Valentina Kirlian, electrophotography was originally hailed as a window into the unknown, a way to see the "unseeable," which could revolutionize our concept of ourselves and the universe. Psychic researchers in the U.S. concluded that the Kirlians had photographed the energy or astral body, thus providing a new technique for exploring the energy body and ESP. Much of the subsequent radiation field photography research has corroborated the earlier findings of the Russian scientists, which has stimulated further interest in the electrophotographic technique.

In our effort to identify the nature of the out-of-body state, and to develop an effective quantifying and monitoring approach, we designed a series of studies in which electrophotography was used to obtain photographic recordings of the right index fingerpad during an induced out-of-body state.

Electrophotography is a type of high voltage photography in which a corona discharge typically appears around the specimen being photographed. Our studies were conducted in an experimental laboratory, with the subject reclining comfortably on a couch and the right index finger resting in a specially designed photographic apparatus, which provided constant control of both finger orientation and pressure applied to

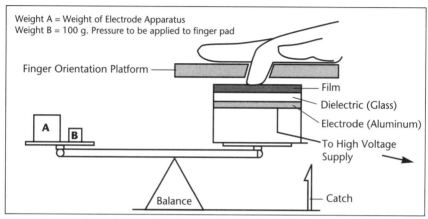

Experimental Arrangement for Electrophotography

This device, developed in our laboratory, allows the experimenter to control both finger orientation and pressure, which is applied to the surface area of the finger as it rests upon film.

**Electrophotographic Apparatus
with Finger Orientation and Pressure Control Device**

A twenty-four-year-old subject rests comfortably on a couch as electrophotographs of the right index finger are obtained.

the fingerpad surface as it rested upon film. All electrical parameters were carefully controlled and held constant for the series of studies.

Our earlier research, including projects funded by the U.S. Army Missile Research and Development Command and the Parapsychology Foundation (New York), found that fingerpad electrophotographic patterns in repeated photographic recordings of individual subjects remained basically stable over a period of several months, with certain corona-discharge characteristics tending to recur at specific locations. These distinguishing characteristics include: *streamers,* in which a stream of energy extends radially from the finger boundary; *symmetry*, in which evenly distributed and symmetrical corona discharge patterns form a perimeter around the fingerpad; *voids,* in which no corona discharge activity occurs; *streamerless points*, in which points of streamer origin are noted but without streamer activity; and *curvatures,* in which an arc tends to mark the boundary for radial movement of the corona discharge. Gender differences were noted, with the electrophotographic patterns for women tending to be more symmetrical and the streamer activity more evenly distributed.

Although pattern stability, sometimes called the *electrophotographic signature*, was noted during the normal or "no-treatment" state for all subjects in our studies, profound changes in corona-discharge activity occurred with the introduction of altered states, including the out-of-

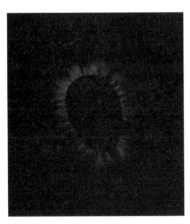

Normal State   Out-of-Body State

Broken-Corona Effect (Twenty-one-year-old male subject)

Normal State   Out-of-Body State

Broken-Corona Effect (Nineteen-year-old female subject)

body state. For all subjects who successfully entered the out-of-body state, the corona-discharge pattern surrounding the right index fingerpad separated to form two distinct parts, a phenomenon we call the *broken-corona effect*. Although our research included investigations of other altered states, such as hypnosis and hypnotic age regression, the broken-corona effect was noted only for the out-of-body state, a finding which suggests that the out-of-body state is unlike other mental and physiological states. This unique effect, which occurred at the point of astral disengagement, characterized only the successful subjects, and continued for the duration of the out-of-body experience. When the out-of-body state ended, the broken-corona effect disappeared, and the electrophotographic pattern returned to normal.

In controlled replication studies, the broken-corona effect was consistently observed during the out-of-body state for subjects of varying ages and background characteristics. As a result of such investigations, we can now objectively monitor the out-of-body state and more effectively develop and evaluate various out-of-body induction and management procedures. Many of the induction procedures and techniques presented earlier in this book were developed in our laboratories under highly controlled conditions, in which the out-of-body experience was carefully monitored using electrophotographic technology.

Occasionally, a feature known as the *remote-image phenomenon* will appear in the electrophotographs of both male and female subjects. This feature is a small but intense point, or cluster-like image, that appears beyond the normal area of corona-discharge activity. Because it appears outside the subject's normal range of electrophotographic pattern, this phenomenon could signal an external astral influence, including the presence of a ministering guide or guardian entity. Only rarely will two remote images appear in the electophotographs, a phenomenon suggesting the presence of two astral entities. It appears plausible that other remote images would appear when the range of electrophotographic recording is expanded. The photographs below illustrate the single remote image phenomenon. Both photographs were taken immediately prior to out-of-body induction.

Interestingly, the remote-image phenomenon occurs with far greater frequency in the photographs of subjects immediately before they enter the out-of-body state. This could be because out-of-body induction procedures typically invoke the presence of astral protection. Possibly in anticipation of that invocation, the astral realm responds even before the out-of-body state is induced. The frequent occurrence of the remote-image phenomenon, with its intense concentration of energy just prior to astral projection, suggests that the astral realm is poised

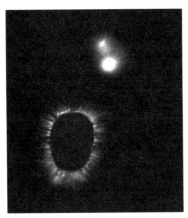 

Remote-Image Phenomena
Appearing in photographs of a twenty-year-old female subject (left), and a twenty-six-year-old male subject (right).

and ready to provide critical support and guidance during the out-of-body experience.

OBEs and Perception

If viewed as a phenomenon in which the astral body is temporarily disengaged from its biological double, the out-of-body state raises crucial questions about the nature of sensory and perceptual experience. Psychic research has clearly demonstrated the human capacity to perceive distant realities independent of known sensory channels. Such an extrasensory capacity, commonly called clairvoyance, would plausibly continue in the detached state of astral projection from the physical body. The out-of-body state of awareness could diminish, or perhaps completely remove the physiological limitations of perception by bypassing our biological mechanisms, thus freeing us to perceive distant realities in a very direct and pronounced super-sensory mode. From that perspective, all out-of-body experiences—which are typically clear and distinct—could be considered extrasensory, in that the out-of-body state requires a separation of the astral from the biological body and its sensory mechanisms. The result is a consciousness liberated from biological constraints.

In our efforts to determine the nature of perception in the out-of-body state, we designed a laboratory study in which experimental subjects in an induced out-of-body state were given the task of identifying an open container of ethyl alcohol which had been placed among other containers in an adjacent laboratory. The volunteer subjects of the study were twenty undergraduate students (ten men and ten women) who had participated in a training program designed to develop skill in entering the out-of-body state at will. The subjects ranged in age from twenty-two to twenty-nine years.

Ten open pint containers, nine of which were filled with water, and one of which was filled with ethyl alcohol, were placed two feet apart on a table in the laboratory. The placement of the containers in numbered positions was determined by a laboratory assistant who was absent for the OBEs exercises and who alone knew the location of the ethyl alcohol container.

Each experimental subject was individually guided into the induced out-of-body state using the OBEs Levitation procedure previously presented in this book. Prior to induction, each subject was instructed to use the out-of-body state as a vehicle to enter the adjacent laboratory and identify through the sense of smell the open container of ethyl alcohol. Upon returning to the normal state, the subjects recorded their response on a record form. Following each trial, the ten containers, all identical in appearance, were randomly rearranged by the laboratory assistant. The trials were conducted once daily for each subject over a five-day period.

On the first trial, seven of the twenty subjects, while in the induced out-of-body state, correctly identified the container of ethyl alcohol. On the second trial, the number increased to eight; and on the third trial, it increased to nine, where it remained for the fourth trial. On the fifth and final trial, ten of the subjects correctly identified the location of the ethyl alcohol container. Four of the twenty subjects correctly identified the container on all five trials; whereas six of the twenty subjects were unsuccessful on all trials.

In follow-up interviews, the successful subjects typically expressed confidence in their ability to enter the out-of-body state, and all reported the capacity to sense the odor of ethyl alcohol while in that state. The unsuccessful subjects were certain neither of their success in achieving the altered state nor of their capacity to specifically sense the odor of ethyl alcohol—though some did report sensing other laboratory odors. Those subjects who were successful on all trials, or who had missed only one of the five trials typically reported a high degree of certainty that they had successfully achieved the out-of-body state, while the subjects who were unsuccessful on all trials typically reported uncertainty. An overall accuracy rate of 43% was observed. The probability of a correct response was .10.

The results of this study suggest that practice in OBEs improves the capacity of subjects to experience the out-of-body state and to perform more accurately on designated out-of-body tasks.

OBEs Case Studies

In addition to controlled laboratory experiments, our research efforts included the analysis of reported OBEs using the case study approach. To date, a total of 283 subjects have submitted detailed reports of spontaneous OBEs. The case files consist of 152 men and 131 women, with an age range of seventeen through fifty-one years. Although some of these individuals reported more than one out-of-body experience, only one instance from each case was randomly selected for this study.

The study analyzed each reported instance of an out-of-body experience and then conducted a follow-up interview with each subject, in an effort to gather additional information about the experience. The results showed:

1. Of the 283 cases analyzed, all indicated that intellectual functions either continued normally or were enhanced in the out-of-body state.

2. A total of 214 subjects reported positive emotions accompanying the experience, including emotions such as joy, tranquillity, and elation. Only 3 persons reported OBEs that were disquieting.

3. The capacity to influence tangible objects—including rearranging or relocating them during the out-of-body experience—was reported in over one-third (103) of the cases. In one instance, the out-of-body traveler, who was a college student, influenced a closet door to close in the dormitory room of a fellow student.

4. Sensory-like experiences during the out-of-body state included 242 instances of weightlessness, 221 instances of hearing, 192 instances of temperature change, 119 instances of touch, 48 instances of smell, and 3 instances of taste. All of the 283 subjects reported instances of sight during the experience.

5. Awareness of a guiding presence accompanying the out-of-body experience was reported by 212 of the 283 subjects. A total of 108 persons reported visible sightings of the presence.

6. Meaningful interactions with other persons occurred frequently in the out-of-body state. Among the 283 cases studied, 11 subjects reported interactions with acquaintances who were also in the out-of-body state. Twenty-seven subjects reported interactions with known persons who were not in the out-of-body state. Forty-one subjects reported interactions with departed friends or relatives. Seven subjects experienced reunions with departed animals.

7. Among the 283 cases analyzed, subjects who were experienced in voluntarily entering the out-of-body state invariably reported more instances of spontaneous out-of-body travel.

8. In 12 instances, the out-of-body experience was believed instrumental in preventing physical injury or other personal misfortune.

9. All 283 cases indicated that the out-of-body state was, by comparison, unlike any other altered state they had experienced.

10. All subjects in this study viewed the out-of-body experience as an invaluable source of insight and knowledge.

Additional analysis of the cases revealed that the emotional state of the subject can be a critical factor in promoting or inhibiting the out-of-body state. Although a relaxed, meditative state tended to facilitate OBEs, the out-of-body state can also occur during intensely stressful states, such as danger, pain, and grief. Out-of-body travel frequently occurred during sleep, with vivid impressions of gliding over terrain or traveling to distant locations.

The Physiology of OBEs

Out-of-body experiences occur only when the astral body disengages from its biological counterpart, a process which seems to be facilitated by a reduction in biological processes and by a peaceful mental state. To determine the specific biological correlates of OBEs, an experimental situation was designed in which various biological measurements were obtained during the out-of-body state.

Ten students, all skilled at voluntarily inducing out-of-body travel, volunteered to participate in the study, which was conducted in a controlled laboratory setting. With each subject resting comfortably on a couch, electromyograph (EMG), galvanic skin response (GSR), brain wave activity (EEG), blood pressure, pulse rate, and right index finger temperature measurements were obtained before, during, and after the out-of-body experience. With the exception of the technician who obtained the physiological measurements, the experimental subject was alone in the laboratory during the experimental session. Along with pre- and post-OBE physiological measurements, ten-minute interval measurements were obtained by the technician for the duration of the out-of-body state. Upon conclusion of the experimental session, the subjects were interviewed to determine their assessment of the experience.

In the post-session interviews, all ten subjects reported success in entering the out-of-body state. The physiological measures obtained indicated marked changes in biological functions for the duration of the out-of-body experience. For all subjects, the recorded changes in EMG indicated a deeply relaxed physical state, while changes in EEG suggested the alpha state. Finger temperature increased for all subjects, while pulse and respiratory rates decreased. These changes occurred early in the out-of-body state, and remained relatively constant for the duration of the experience.

Final measurements obtained upon conclusion of the session indicated a rapid return to the pre-OBE level for all physiological parameters.

Sleep and OBEs

Certain characteristics of the sleep state appear particularly conducive to OBEs. With the physical body at rest, the biological constraints that could inhibit astral travel to distant destinations are relaxed. As discussed in a previous chapter, one view of OBEs holds that sleep itself is an out-of-body state, and that many of our so-called "dream experiences" are literally OBEs.

Whether sleep is an out-of-body state, or simply an altered state conducive to out-of-body travel, it remains plausible that strategies could be developed to facilitate OBEs and out-of-body travel to desired destinations during sleep. To investigate that possibility, we developed a study in which certain pre-sleep strategies were applied to induce OBEs during sleep. The major purpose of the study was twofold: first, to investigate the effectiveness of the pre-sleep strategies in promoting highly specific OBEs, and second, to determine the validity of the out-of-body experience itself.

The subjects of the study were twenty college student volunteers (ten men and ten women), all dormitory residents, whose ages ranged from eighteen to twenty-four years. The subjects had completed at least one college-level course in parapsychology that had included practice in inducing the out-of-body state. All of the subjects had experienced the induced out-of-body state and successful out-of-body travel to a distant location.

The participants of the study were instructed to induce out-of-body travel through pre-sleep autosuggestion, and while in the out-of-body state, to identify an object that had been placed by a research assistant on a table centrally located in the college's parapsychology laboratory. The identity of the object was known only to the research assistant, who had selected it randomly from nine other objects, none of which had been seen either by the project investigator or by the subjects. The pre-sleep autosuggestions, which were presented in the normal sleep environment just prior to falling asleep on a designated date, consisted of the following:

> *As I sleep, I will be free to travel to the laboratory and view the object which has been placed on a table in the center of the room. Upon awakening, I will have full recall of the out-of-body experience.*

Images of the laboratory and its location on campus were then formed, and additional autosuggestions directing travel to it were presented as sleep ensued.

Immediately upon awakening, participants in the study recorded their out-of-body travel experiences in detail. Analysis of the results of the study indicated that all subjects appeared to be successful in entering the out-of-body state. All reported having successfully entered the laboratory. A total of eight men and seven women successfully identified the critical elements of the previously unseen object—an artist-signed jade carving of two horses, in shades of green and pale lavender, mounted on an ebony base. Three of the remaining five subjects identified the jade carving but were unsuccessful in identifying the object's other critical elements. The remaining two subjects were unsuccessful in identifying any of the object's critical elements.

In a replication of the study using a second population of twenty subjects, all conditions were held constant, with the exception of a different object—a model train with four boxcars and a caboose. As in the previous study, all subjects reported successfully entering the out-of-body state and traveling out-of-body to the laboratory. However, only six men and four women correctly identified the object and its essential elements. Amazingly, however, three men and two women successfully identified the train's manufacturer, which was printed in white letters on the side of the engine.

These results are sufficient to suggest that out-of-body travel during sleep could be deliberately induced to access highly specific information not otherwise available to us.

OBEs During Sleep

The extent of spontaneous out-of-body travel during sleep is unknown. Many persons recall frequent travel, and some report that it is a nightly occurrence. Others, however, never recall experiencing the phenomenon.

Some skilled out-of-body travelers report success in voluntarily directing out-of-body travel during sleep to desired destinations with a variety of induction and management procedures. The purpose of the following three-phase study was twofold: first, to explore the procedures used by successful subjects to induce out-of-body travel during sleep, and second, to develop an effective procedure for stimulating OBEs during sleep.

In Phase I of the study, fifteen volunteer college students (nine men and six women), all of whom had reported success in utilizing the sleep state to induce out-of-body travel, were interviewed to gather information concerning the techniques they used. All of the subjects, whose ages ranged from twenty-one through twenty-nine, had acquired advanced skill in astral traveling to target destinations independently of the sleep state. Following is a summary of the interview results:

1. Physical relaxation, a serene mental state, and motivation were considered the essential prerequisites to successful astral travel during sleep. A clear intent to travel out-of-body was formulated immediately prior to falling asleep.

2. All subjects used autosuggestion during the drowsy state just prior to falling asleep. The suggestions varied, but typically included such suggestions as:

   I am now ready to leave my body. I am free to go wherever I wish. I will be fully protected as I travel. I will return with ease whenever I decide to do so.

3. For travel to designated destinations, images of the destination were formed by the subjects and integrated into the drowsy state preceding sleep.

In Phase II of the study, the interview results of Phase I were analyzed, and a procedure was developed to stimulate out-of-body travel during sleep. The procedure, called *Transitional Travel*, was designed to give the sleeping subject greater control in traveling to desired destinations. The procedure emphasizes relaxation, empowering affirmations, and imagery to induce the out-of-body state and facilitate easy travel. (See Chapter Six for the complete five-step procedure.)

In Phase III of the study, a second volunteer population of twenty-two subjects (fourteen men and eight women), none of whom had reported success in utilizing sleep as a vehicle for out-of-body travel, were given training in Transitional Travel. During the training period, which consisted of one-hour sessions daily over a five-day period, all subjects reported success in entering the out-of-body state. Upon completion of the training period, the subjects were instructed to use the procedure and record their out-of-body experiences nightly for a two-week period. The travel records were analyzed at the end of the two-week period to determine the frequency of out-of-body travel among the subjects.

The following is a summary of the results of Phase III:

1. Eighteen of the twenty-two subjects reported at least one out-of-body travel experience during the two-week period. Of the remaining four subjects, two were undecided about whether they had traveled out-of-body during the experimental period, and two believed they had not traveled out-of-body during that period.

2. Sixteen of the twenty-two subjects reported successful out-of-body travel to at least one designated destination during the two-week period.

3. A total of nine subjects reported at least one out-of-body experience for each night of the study.

4. Seven of the subjects reported multiple OBEs on each night of the study.

5. All of the successful subjects reported improvement in their ability to voluntarily enter the out-of-body state.

This study, although subjective, suggests that skill in initiating and directing out-of-body travel during sleep can be acquired through practice and experience using laboratory-developed procedures.

Self-Induced OBEs: A Survey of Successful Subjects

Objective analysis of self-induced OBEs and the conditions related to them is important in our study of this complex phenomenon, because it increases our understanding of the induction process, and suggests ways to master it. The purpose of the following study was twofold: first, to determine the personal characteristics associated with successful self-induction of the out-of-body state; and second, to determine the specific techniques used by successful subjects.

Subjects of the study were eighteen volunteer students (seven men and eleven women) who reported frequent self-induced OBEs, and who had successfully demonstrated their self-induction skills in a controlled laboratory setting. The subjects were instructed to write a two-part narrative describing themselves and the techniques they used for inducing OBEs, with particular attention given to the following:

PART I

1. Describe your present health status.
2. To what degree are you in control of your life?
3. Describe the psychological state that typically characterizes your life.
4. How would your rate your academic performance?
5. How would your friends typically describe you?

PART II

1. What are the potential benefits of OBEs?
2. Describe specifically the techniques you use to induce the out-of-body state.
3. What are some situational or personal factors that could make induction of the out-of-body state difficult?

Analysis of the narrative contents of the responses revealed the following:

All of the subjects described themselves as either healthy or reasonably healthy and in control of their lives.

The subjects' descriptions of their psychological state were typically positive. Among their specific descriptions were *well-adjusted, balanced, secure, self-confident, happy, motivated,* and *flexible.*

All of the subjects rated their academic performance as above average. Three of the subjects rated their performance as excellent, and two subjects rated their performance as superior. The remaining subjects rated their performance as either high or very high.

All participants of the study gave highly positive pictures of themselves as described by their friends. The most frequent characteristic noted in their descriptions was *genuine* (fourteen instances). Other characteristics were *independent* (twelve instances), *responsible* (eleven instances), *honest* (nine instances), *sincere* (nine instances), *hard-working* (three instances), *determined* (three instances), and *fun-loving* (two instances). Negative descriptions, although rare, included three instances of *headstrong*, three instances of *inconsistent*, and one instance of *self-centered*.

The reported benefits of OBEs included the following:

1. They are relaxing.
2. They are a source of important insight.
3. They provide quality solutions to problems.
4. They are a source of pleasure.
5. They are gratifying and personally fulfilling.
6. They add excitement to life.
7. They are motivating.
8. They stimulate creative thinking.
9. They restore physical and mental balance.
10. They build self-confidence and self-esteem.
11. They promote intellectual efficiency.

The induction techniques practiced by the eighteen subjects had several common characteristics. Early in the induction process, physical relaxation, mental imagery, and affirmation were used by all the subjects. Imagining a glow of protective energy enveloping the physical body was used by twelve of the eighteen subjects. A shaft of light upon which the astral body was borne away from the physical was envisioned by seven of the eighteen subjects. Affirmation and imagery were used by all subjects to direct travel to particular destinations. Invoking the presence of an astral guide to provide protection and direction during out-of-body travel was used by sixteen of the eighteen subjects.

Fourteen of the subjects reported previous practice in various meditation strategies. Strategies utilizing the sleep state were used by seven subjects. Each subject of the study reported having successfully used more than one induction procedure.

The reported situational or personal factors that interfered with successful induction of the out-of-body state included noise distractions, physical discomfort, the presence of others, and time constrictions.

Taken together, the results of this study suggest that a positive mental state, a strong sense of personal control, and a healthy self-image are critical to the success of out-of-body self-induction efforts. Imagery, affirmation, and relaxation were prominent elements in the induction procedures used by all subjects in the study.

Spontaneous Versus Induced OBEs:
A Comparative Analysis

Personal accounts of OBEs have suggested that spontaneous as well as voluntarily induced OBEs are potentially empowering. Previous research, however, has not sufficiently explored the comparative values of these two categories of psychic experience. This study was, consequently, designed to assess the empowerment significance of spontaneous versus experimentally induced OBEs.

Since the empowering value of OBEs may not always be immediately known to the individual, this present study included the experimental subjects' assessments of their past spontaneous OBEs as well as their immediate and delayed assessments of their experimentally induced OBEs.

Ten volunteer college students (five men and five women), all of whom had reported more than one previous out-of-body experience, participated in the study. The age range of the subjects was nineteen through twenty-six years.

The project was conducted in a quiet laboratory setting. Each subject first evaluated the empowering significance of previous spontaneous OBEs from *not significant* to *highly significant* on the following 5-point scale:

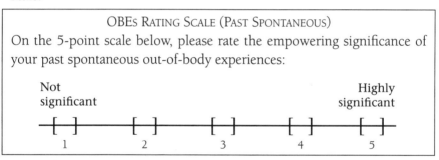

Seven of the 10 subjects in the study rated their previous spontaneous OBEs as *highly significant* (point 5 on the 5-point scale), with the remaining three subjects rating their past OBEs experience at point 4 on the rating scale, thus resulting in an overall average rating of 4.7 for the previous spontaneous experience.

Each subject, while resting comfortably on a couch, was then guided into an induced out-of-body state by the researcher, who used the OBEs

Levitation procedure presented in Chapter Three. Upon conclusion of the induced experience, each subject evaluated the significance of the experience from *not significant* to *highly significant* on the same 5-point scale.

Immediately following the induced OBE, five of the 10 subjects rated the experience as *highly significant* (Point 5 on the rating scale). The remaining 5 subjects rated the experience at point 4. The resulting overall average rating immediately following the induced state was 4.5, a figure somewhat below that found for previous spontaneous experiences.

Four weeks later, each subject returned to the laboratory and again evaluated the OBE that had been induced the previous month from *not significant* to *highly significant* on the 5-point scale. The questionnaire read:

> Four weeks ago, you were a volunteer participant in our induced out-of-body study. Please rate your present opinion of the empowering significance of that experience on the 5-point scale below.

The ratings obtained four weeks after the induced experience increased to the level of those for the past spontaneous OBEs, with an overall average rating of 4.7 on the 5-point scale.

Although the population for this study was limited to 10 subjects, the results suggest that experimentally induced OBEs are potentially as empowering as spontaneous OBEs; however the empowering significance of the experimentally induced experience may not always be immediately apparent to the subject.

Induced OBEs: The Effects of Past Experience

The primary goal of the following study was twofold: first, to develop an out-of-body induction strategy based on the reported induction techniques used by experienced subjects; and second, to evaluate the effectiveness of that induction procedure with both experienced and inexperienced subjects. The participants in the study were ten subjects who had reported success in inducing the out-of-body state at will, and ten subjects who had no reported success in inducing the out-of-body state. The age range of the experienced subjects was nineteen through twenty-seven years, and the age range of the inexperienced subjects was eighteen through twenty-six years.

The subjects, all volunteers, were oriented in a group session concerning the nature of the research project, as well as the theory and dynamics of the out-of-body state. The ten experienced subjects were then asked to write a report identifying the techniques they used to induce the out-of-body state. After analysis of the written reports, an interview was conducted with each experienced subject to gain further information about their induction procedures and techniques. The inexperienced subjects were also interviewed and provided any needed clarification of the research effort.

Based on analysis of the interviews with the experienced subjects, common induction elements were identified, and an OBEs induction procedure was developed. The procedure was later used with each subject in both groups to induce the out-of-body state.

Prior to out-of-body induction, each participant in the study was escorted to an art studio in another campus building, where they viewed an easel, already positioned, but without a painting. A painting was later placed on the easel, by a research assistant who alone selected the painting and who alone knew its essential features. The experimental task required each subject to return out-of-body to the art studio and view the painting, giving particular attention to its essential features.

The out-of-body sessions were conducted in a quiet laboratory setting with soft, indirect lighting, while the subject reclined comfortably on a couch. The induction script, which included elements compiled from the reports of the successful OBEs subjects, was then presented, as follows:

> In this experiment, your task is to leave your body and view a painting on an easel situated in the center of the art studio. When you return to your body, you will be asked to describe the essential features of the painting.
>
> With your eyes now closed, let yourself become more and more comfortable and relaxed. As you slow your breathing and relax your body, you are at complete peace, confident of your ability to leave your body. You are surrounded by radiant and protective energy as you now prepare to leave your body. As you travel outside your body, you will be safe and secure.

You are now in complete control as you begin to drift slowly, very slowly away from your body. You can feel yourself slipping upward from your body. Looking back, you can now see your body at rest. You can return to your body at any moment simply by deciding to do so.

Now disengaged from your physical body, you are free to travel to the art studio, where you will view the selected painting. Upon viewing the painting, you will let yourself return to your physical body with comfort and ease. You have as much time as you need to travel to the studio and view the painting.

Upon conclusion of the induction exercise, adequate time was allowed for out-of-body travel. The duration of the out-of-body session was timed and recorded for each subject. Timing began at the conclusion of the induction instructions, and ended when the subjects opened their eyes.

For the experienced subjects, the duration of the out-of-body experience ranged from 6 minutes, 17 seconds to 11 minutes, 48 seconds, with an average time of 9 minutes, 22 seconds. For the inexperienced group, the duration of the out-of-body experience ranged from 5 minutes, 40 seconds to l4 minutes, 52 seconds, with an average of 10 minutes, 31 seconds.

The painting depicted a man on a horse in a rainstorm. Eight of the ten experienced subjects included a horse in their descriptions of the painting's essential elements. Five of the experienced subjects also included the remaining two essential elements—the rider and the rainstorm—in their descriptions. Two of the experienced subjects identified none of the painting's essential elements, although they did include minor aspects of the painting, such as certain colors and landscape features.

Two of the inexperienced subject included all the essential elements in their descriptions. One of the inexperienced subjects mentioned only the horse and rider, and three subjects mentioned only the horse. The four remaining inexperienced subjects included none of the painting's essential elements in their descriptions.

Among the subjects who showed only limited success in identifying the painting's essential elements, the horse was the most commonly identified element. This was probably due to the central position of the horse, rearing in fright and partially concealing the rider. The least frequently identified element for both groups was the storm, a background feature.

Although the results of this experiment could have been influenced by clairvoyance, bi-location, or some other form of ESP, the successful subjects described the experience as distinctively out-of-body in nature and attributed their success to out-of-body travel.

The results of this study suggest that previous out-of-body experience could improve performance in the experimental setting. However, since the induction procedure was drawn from the reports of the experienced subjects, it would seem to follow that the familiar procedure would work better for that group. The inexperienced group not only identified fewer essential elements, but also introduced more extraneous material in their descriptions of the painting. Nevertheless, the procedure did result in considerable success for the inexperienced group as well, a finding that suggests the usefulness of this induction procedure as a teaching tool.

Precognition and OBEs

Practice and experience are essential to learning, including the development of our psychic faculties. The purpose of this two-phase study was, first, to investigate the precognitive performance of subjects who had completed a training program in precognition, and second, to explore the relative effectiveness of various precognitive strategies, including OBEs.

Phase I of this study investigated the precognitive success rate of thirty-six subjects who had six months of previous experience in study group activities designed to develop their precognitive skills. During this phase, the group met bi-monthly over a period of six months. During that period, the group generated 287 predictions, with a documented accuracy rate of 63 percent. Many of the predictions related to group participants and were personal in nature. Among the validated predictions were an automobile accident involving the daughter of a group member, a job promotion for a government employee in the group, and a certificate of achievement recognizing the community services of a teacher in the group. The high accuracy rate of the predictions suggested that something beyond chance was at work in the group's efforts.

Upon conclusion of Phase I of the study, twenty-seven participants in the phase volunteered to participate in Phase II, which became known as the *Psi Span Project*. The project was initiated to gather precognitive information over a two-year period through the application of three experimental group techniques: the out-of-body experience, hypnosis, and objectology, which involves the use of inanimate objects as precognitive tools. The project emphasized objective assessment and careful documentation.

The Psi Span Project consisted of three precognitive groups and a validation committee. The precognitive groups were each assigned one of three precognitive procedures: 1) out-of-body; 2) hypnosis; and 3) objectology. The membership of each group consisted of nine participants. The procedures of each group were relatively fixed, with each group meeting monthly to gather and record precognitive data. An appointed recorder for each group assembled the predictive data and submitted it to the validation committee of twelve members, who assumed responsibility for the validation efforts. The committee submitted monthly reports that provided validation results.

The objectives of each group, in addition to gathering predictive data, included refining their respective precognitive strategies. The out-of-body group attempted to develop out-of-body strategies that could extend awareness into the future during the out-of-body state; the hypnosis group attempted to perfect an age progression technique in which the future could be objectively viewed or subjectively experienced; and the objectology group attempted to perfect their precognitive skills using pendulum, crystal gazing, and table tilting. Throughout the project, flexibility and experimentation in a permissive and relaxed environment were emphasized, along with careful recordkeeping.

Over the two-year period from September 1, 1990, to September 1, 1992, the three groups assembled a total of 342 predictions. As of January 1, 1996, a total of 253 of those predictions had been validated. The predictions of the three groups ranged from highly personal matters to predictions of national and international significance. The following table presents a breakdown of each precognitive group's total predictions and validation results.

Psi Span Strategies and Precognitive Performance		
Group	*Total Predictions*	*% Validated*
I. Out-of-body	31	81
II. Hypnosis	101	78
III. Objectology	210	66

Compared to the validation results for Phase I of the study, each group showed improvement. Although the out-of-body group reported the lowest number of predictions, they obtained the highest validation results. Since the predictions generated by the three groups reach beyond the year 2000, the number of validated predictions for each group is expected to increase as the validation effort continues.

OBEs and the Near-Death Experience (NDE)

One of the most commonly reported effects of OBEs is a sense of increased personal power. Similarly, persons who report having a *near-death experience* (NDE) almost invariably view it as profoundly empowering. The purpose of the following study was to explore the empowering benefits of the two experiences through structured interviews with persons who had experienced both the out-of-body experience and the near-death experience.

Eighteen persons (eight women and ten men) who reported having experienced both OBEs and near-death experiences volunteered for the study. The age range of the subjects was from twenty-seven through fifty-eight years. Four of the subjects reported near-death experiences resulting from traffic accidents, three from sports-related accidents, two from heart attacks, two from injuries sustained in a fall, two from injuries sustained in military combat, two from near-drowning, one from on-the-job exposure to an industrial chemical, one from an accidental drug overdose, and one from a plane crash. Although eleven of the subjects reported having experienced the voluntarily induced out-of-body state, only spontaneous OBEs were used for comparison.

The subjects were interviewed using the following interview guide, which was specifically developed for the study:

NDE/OBEs INTERVIEW GUIDE

1. What were the conditions surrounding your near-death experience?

2. Describe your near-death experience.

3. How did the near-death experience affect your life?

4. What were the conditions surrounding your out-of-body experience(s)?

5. Describe your out-of-body experience(s).

6. How did the out-of-body experience(s) affect your life?

7. How were your near-death and out-of-body experience(s) alike? How were they different?

Upon completion of the interviews, the subjects were instructed to write a detailed description, in which they compared and contrasted their near-death and out-of-body experiences.

Analysis of the interview results and the subjects' written descriptions of their experiences revealed certain similarities and differences in the two categories of experiences. The similarities included:

1. All subjects reported that both the near-death experience and the out-of-body experience were personally meaningful and significant.

2. All subjects viewed the experiences, whether near-death or out-of-body, as purposeful and empowering.

3. Both categories of experiences were typically described as mystical or spiritual in nature.

4. Impressions of floating and ascending were noted by all subjects for both categories.

5. All subjects reported sharpened perceptions accompanying both categories.

6. Increased insight and tranquillity were specified as enduring consequences of both categories.

Differences reported were:

1. Compared to OBEs, NDEs were described as more intense, and their effects as more long-term.

2. All the subjects reported that the near-death experience influenced their perception of life, and the meaning of life after death.

3. All subjects reported significant life changes following the near-death experience. Examples included changes in personal values, family relationships, and careers. The changes associated with OBEs were also described as significant—but were typically less dramatic and more progressive in nature.

4. The near-death experience was more likely to be seen as spiritually profound. Significant interactions with higher planes occurred in both states, but were more intense during the near-death experience.

5. Interactions with known discarnates occurred in both states, but with greater frequency during the near-death experience.

6. Awareness of a brilliant dimension of pure light and significant interactions with angels or ministering guides occurred in both states, but were more likely to occur during the near-death experience.

Hopefully, future research into these complex phenomena will enhance our understanding of the nature of our existence, and suggest new ways to enrich and empower our lives.

11

A Seven-Day Developmental Plan for OBEs

Growth is the only evidence of life.

John Henry Newman, *Apologia pro Vita Sua*

I N OUR STUDY of OBEs, we have explored many ways to enrich our lives with new insight and power. OBEs manifest our capacity to stretch our present limits of awareness, reach beyond the ordinary, and access distant sources of growth and enlightenment.

By developing our out-of-body potential, we discover new meaning to our present existence, and the magnificent realities that lie ahead of us. Each out-of-body experience is a promissory note that assures us of our immortality, not simply as a nebulous energy system, but as a conscious entity whose evolution is a never-ending marvel. Becoming psychically empowered, however, requires an organized effort and a firm commitment to make the best of our lives and develop our potential to it peak.

The *Seven-Day Developmental Plan for OBEs* presented here is formulated to activate a new growth spiral and unleash our highest growth potential. For easy reference, the plan includes certain strategies previously presented in this book, and organizes them into a systematic approach that recognizes the progressive nature of personal empowerment. The plan is flexible, and can be enriched by the addition of strategies found elsewhere in this book.

159

For each day, the plan identifies an objective, and presents relevant activities for achieving it. Beginning with simple practice and conditioning exercises, the plan progresses to more complex strategies, and finally culminates in out-of-body travel to the highest realms of cosmic power.

This seven-day plan provides a starting point for a future filled with excitement, discovery, and unlimited growth possibilities.

Day One

Objective: *To generate a mental and physical state of readiness conducive to out-of-body travel.*

Day one of our psychic empowerment plan introduces four exercises specifically designed to promote out-of-body readiness.

Astral Meditation

This procedure uses a shiny object, such as a crystal or a lighted candle, to build the concentration skills required for inducing OBEs. Here is the procedure:

Step 1. Center your attention for a few moments on the shiny object, then slowly expand your peripheral vision to its limits, taking in as much of your surroundings as possible. Almost immediately you will notice a white glow forming throughout your visual field.

Step 2. Close your eyes, slow your breathing, and mentally scan your body from your head to your feet, relaxing each muscle as you go.

Step 3. With your body fully relaxed, envision yourself fully enveloped by a white glow of positive, radiant energy.

Step 4. Affirm: *I am at peace with myself and the universe. I am balanced mentally, physically, and spiritually. I am infused with positive energy.*

Step 5: Resolution. Conclude the meditation by reflecting on the experience and mentally reaffirming the empowering effects of the exercise.

Moon View

This procedure requires comfortably focusing for a few minutes on the moon, preferably a full moon, and then, with your eyes closed, imagining yourself literally visiting the moon and exploring its craters, planes, and caverns. Let yourself become so absorbed in the experience that you seem to experience firsthand the moon's tangible presence. You can envision yourself holding a moon rock, or letting moon sand filter through your fingers. If the moon is not available for viewing, close your eyes and create a mental picture of the moon.

In-Body Travel

This procedure exercises the mind's capacity to create and remove physical sensations. Here is the complete procedure:

Step 1. Let yourself become comfortable and relaxed, then, with your eyes closed, select a small body area—a hand, finger, or toe—and center your full attention on that specific area's physical sensations.

Step 2. Continue to focus your full attention on the selected area, and practice creating and removing new sensations, such as warmth, numbness, tingling, and pressure in that specific body area.

Step 3. Conclude the procedure by allowing your mind to become passive as all physical sensations return to a state of rest.

Creative Imagery

This practice exercise is particularly effective in promoting readiness for astral travel to distant destinations. Here is the procedure:

Step 1. Think of your favorite place and imagine that you are there. Focus your full attention on this special place, noting in detail your surroundings and your sense of serenity and peace.

Step 2. Shift your attention to peaceful images of objects drifting in space. Examples are slow-moving clouds, a leaf in the breeze, or a magic carpet.

Step 3. Select a particular object in motion and imagine that it is a transportation vehicle. Envision yourself as its lone passenger on a journey to a special destination.

Step 4. Mentally visit any destination of your choice, or simply allow your imaginary journey to unfold spontaneously.

Step 5. Shift your attention away from your journey and back to your present surroundings. Reflect on the experience and its empowering effects.

These practice procedures exercise our ability to reach beyond the confines of the biological body, and prepare us mentally and physically for out-of-body travel.

Day Two

Objective: *To experience out-of-body travel to distant destinations.*

Day two of our plan introduces two out-of-body induction procedures. The first procedure, *OBEs Levitation*, uses impressions of physical weightlessness, followed by imagery of the biological body levitating and then returning to its original position, while the astral body remains in the levitated state, poised to travel to distant destinations. The second procedure, *Transitional Travel*, exercises our capacity to travel out-of-body during sleep.

OBEs Levitation

This procedure requires only sensations of biological levitation, not actual levitation. The rationale for this procedure is that sensations of biological levitation can release the astral body from the physical body, thereby producing astral levitation. Here is the eight-step procedure:

Step 1. While in a comfortable, reclining position, mentally scan your entire body, pausing at areas of tension and letting them relax. Slow your breathing, taking a little longer to exhale, until you develop a relaxed, effortless breathing pattern.

Step 2. Focus your full attention on your physical body and imagine it becoming lighter and lighter, until it finally seems to become weightless.

Step 3. As the sense of weightlessness continues, imagine your physical body, as light as a feather, beginning to rise slowly. Next, envision your physical body momentarily suspended in space, then slowly returning to its original position—leaving your consciousness behind in astral body form, still suspended over your physical body.

Step 4. From overhead, view your physical body which is now resting comfortably below. Notice your sense of weightlessness and separation from your physical body.

Step 5. Invoke the positive energies of higher astral planes by envisioning your projected astral body as well as your physical body below surrounded by white radiance, then affirming:

My total being is now enveloped in the powerful radiance of cosmic energy. As I travel, I will be empowered and protected, mentally, physically, and spiritually, by the positive energies of higher astral planes. I will return to my physical body at any time by simple intent alone.

Step 6. Give yourself permission to travel to any pre-determined destination, or simply allow travel to unfold effortlessly and spontaneously. Make in-flight corrections as needed, by consciously intervening in the out-of-body experience. Reaffirm periodically that powerful cosmic energy is infusing your total being, including your physical body as it rests safely at a distance.

Step 7. To return to your physical body, envision it in its familiar setting, then simply affirm your intent to return to it. Once in the presence of your physical body passively at rest, give yourself permission to reunite with it. Upon re-engaging your body, notice your breathing and other physical sensations.

Step 8. Conclude the procedure with a brief period of rest and reflection. Give particular attention to the empowering benefits of the experience.

Transitional Travel

This procedure is designed to promote out-of-body travel during sleep and give you greater control of the experience. Here is the five-step procedure:

Step 1: Preparation. Just before falling asleep, relax your entire body by mentally scanning it and releasing all tension. Focus on slowing your breathing. Suggest to yourself that time is slowing down.

Step 2: Affirmation. Affirm that, as your sleep, you will slip out of your body and travel to a distant destination. Selecting a specific destination is optional. Invoke higher plane protection and the empowering presence of ministering guides by affirming: *I am fully protected and secure as I travel out-of-body.*

Step 3: Mental Imagery. Envision your astral body as a vaporous form rising from your physical body as sleep ensues. In that projected state, view your physical body at rest enveloped in a protective glow, and allow your astral being to float farther away from your body.

Step 4: Astral Travel. Flow spontaneously into distant realities or travel deliberately to a predetermined destination. For specific destinations, envision the destination and reaffirm your intent to experience it. Give yourself permission to gain knowledge and power from the experience.

Step 5: Re-entry. Conclude the astral adventure by returning at will to rejoin your physical body. At this point, you may choose either to awaken from sleep or to allow sleep to continue uninterrupted.

Day Three

Objective: *To experience distant cosmic realms through out-of-body travel.*
Day three of our OBEs plan introduces *Astral Surfing*, an out-of-body method which uses very flexible induction and management procedures. It emphasizes spontaneous out-of-body exploration of the cosmos, without structured limits or specifically defined goals. It is broad in scope and offers a sweeping array of growth options. It is based on the premise that consciousness in the out-of-body state can scan the universe, surf the rich astral planes, and discover new realms of pleasure and power. Like other out-of-body experience procedures, Astral Surfing requires a quiet, comfortable setting free of distractions. Here is the procedure:

Step 1: Preliminary Considerations. A period of at least one hour, during which brief, periodic re-engagements of the physical body can occur, is recommended for surfing. These transient re-entries provide brief rest periods within a series of flights, while enhancing the effectiveness of surfing and preventing post-flight fatigue. Invocations that assure complete cosmic protection through affirmations and imagery of being encased in light are recommended at the beginning, and periodically throughout the procedure.

Step 2: Induction. To induce the out-of-body state, settle back and let your physical body become progressively relaxed as your thoughts become increasingly passive. Envision an astral flight vehicle—such as a crystalline capsule or carpet of energy—bearing your consciousness in astral body form upward and away from your physical body to facilitate induction of the out-of-body state. Imagery of the flight vehicle is likewise effective for periodic re-entries and reinduction following rest intervals.

Step 3: Surfing. To initiate surfing, envision the three-dimensional cosmic design of the universe, with flight pathways among cosmic points, dimensions, and planes. Points in the cosmic design signify brilliant concentrations of cosmic energy, with the colors of a given point denoting its particular power capacities—such as green for healing, yellow for intellectual power, and blue for serenity. Cosmic points can be aligned along an inviting surfing thoroughfare, or they can exist as isolated concentrations of bright, interacting energies.

In contrast to points, cosmic dimensions are large domains of energy in the cosmic design, glowing and radiating power. Dimensions vary in size, color, intensity, and shape. Some are so distant that they are barely visible to the astral eye, while others dominate the cosmic structure. Certain expansive dimensions embody constellations of bright cosmic points and planes, while others emit only a soft, inviting cosmic glow.

Cosmic planes are represented by layers of radiant energy in the cosmic design, with each layer differing in design and color. Certain planes appear rugged and irregular, while others are smooth and elegant. Some planes exist as components of complex astral dimensions, while others appear apart from other cosmic elements. Like certain cosmic dimensions, some planes seem almost impenetrable, while others challenge contact and interaction.

Surfing among points, dimensions, and planes can be either spontaneous or destination-oriented. Spontaneous surfing occurs effortlessly and requires no astral itinerary or flight plan. You can glide freely in and out of planes and dimensions, stopping at will, then moving on to other destinations. You can interface cosmic points to draw energy from them, or slip into dimensions and planes to access their empowering properties whenever needed. In contrast to spontaneous surfing, destination-oriented surfing requires deliberately choosing particular pathways as travel routes to designated dimensions, points, or planes.

Step 4: Astral Return. To end out-of-body travel, envision your physical body in its familiar setting, and affirm your intent to return to it. A sense of presence in the body, accompanied by specific physical sensations signals a successful re-entry. This procedure is effective for transient re-entries during Astral Surfing, as well as the final astral return.

Step 5: Conclusion. Conclude Astral Surfing by briefly reviewing the experience and reflecting on its empowering effects.

Day Four

Objective: *To access the cosmic sources of healing and rejuvenation.*
Day four of our plan introduces the *PK Pool of Power*, one of the most effective out-of-body procedures for achieving health-related goals, such as fortifying the immune system, slowing the rate of aging, managing pain, and promoting healing, to list but a few of the procedure's health benefits. A period of approximately one hour should be set aside for the eight-step procedure to be conducted in a quiet, safe place. Here is the procedure:

Step 1. While resting in a comfortable, reclining position, with your legs uncrossed and your hands resting comfortably at your sides, take a few deep breaths, then develop a slow, rhythmic breathing pattern. Focus for a few minutes only on your breathing. Remind yourself that you are safe, comfortable, and secure. Invoke the empowering presence of higher astral influences, by envisioning yourself surrounded by radiant light.

Step 2. Center your attention on your forehead, and slowly allow your thoughts to turn inward. Allow any darkness or shades of gray to become progressively brighter, until you experience only radiant white light. Envision your astral body as a radiant light form slowly rising from your physical body along with your conscious awareness. As you rise over your body, notice your sense of freedom and serenity. As you ascend gently upward, you are at perfect peace. Remind yourself that you are infused with light and protected by the highest influences of the cosmos. At any time, you can return to your body with ease upon deciding to do so.

Step 3. Now liberated from your biological body, you are free to travel wherever you wish. The distant reaches of the universe are now at your command. The highest dimensions and farthest planes invite your contact and interaction.

Step 4. As you sense a wondrous communion with the cosmos, turn your attention to a distant, crystalline plane glowing with pure energy. If you do not immediately identify the crystalline plane, continue scanning the cosmos until it comes into view, then let yourself be drawn to it. Upon entering the plane, you are immediately enveloped and invigorated by the warmth of its powerful energy.

Step 5. At the innermost region of the plane lies a crystal clear pool, calmly reflecting the sparkling radiance of the surrounding plane. Approaching the pool, you can sense the vastness of its power. Drawn by its amazing beauty, you plunge into the pool, probing its fathomless depths and limitless boundaries. As you explore the incredible pool, you sense a powerful infusion of invigorating energy.

Step 6. Upon ascending out of the pool, you notice a beautiful, bejeweled chalice resting on a crystal pedestal at the pool's edge. Gazing in amazement at its intricate workmanship and exquisite beauty, you take the chalice from the pedestal and fill it with water from the pool. Lifting the chalice and pouring its water over your body, you are thrilled with fantastic pleasure as the water flows sensuously downward. Your entire being is saturated with power. The vast riches of the universe are now at your command. Remind yourself that whatever you desire can now be yours.

Step 7. Lifting the chalice toward the universe, affirm: *My thoughts and images are the language of the cosmos.* State your goals, envision them, and affirm them as present realities. If, for instance, your goals are health-related, state each goal specifically, envision that particular body part or system functioning normally, and affirm that the goal has been achieved.

Step 8. You are now ready to return the chalice to its place on the pedestal, and reunite with your physical body. Notice your body at rest and sense yourself gently re-engaging it. Upon re-entry, but before opening your eyes, take a few moments to reflect on the experience and to reaffirm its empowering effects.

Day Five

Objective: *To retrieve past-life experiences and glean empowering knowledge from them.*

Day five of our plan introduces *Past-Life Ascent*, a structured, step-by-step approach that uses both hypnosis and the out-of-body state. This procedure views past life as a three-dimensional phenomenon: Pre-incarnate life is our existence prior to our first incarnation; incarnate life is our existence as incarnates in each lifetime; and discarnate life is our existence as discarnates between lifetimes. The goal of Past-Life Ascent is cosmic ascension and raised consciousness, in which past-life awareness reaches its peak.

Like other out-of-body procedures, Past-Life Ascent requires a quiet, comfortable setting. Approximately one hour, during which there are absolutely no interruptions, should be set aside for the session. Here is the six-step procedure:

Step 1: Goal Formulation. Formulate your personal objectives and state them as specifically as possible. Your objectives may simply be to practice the procedure and develop your induction skills. On the other hand, you may wish to conduct a comprehensive overview of your past lives, or to investigate a particular past lifetime in-depth. Your goal may be to explore past-life experiences that relate to a particular present situation, or to identify past-life themes or patterns, such as recurring relationships, careers, or commitments. You may wish to explore past-life tasks you can now complete, or past-life problems you can now solve. You may decide to explore your earliest pre-incarnate existence, or specific discarnate intervals between your past lives. You may wish to identify your most recent past lifetime, or to re-experience your very earliest incarnation. You may decide to explore your past-life experiences in a given geographic region or within a particular culture. Your goal may be to discover important knowledge gained in a previous life but presently lost to conscious awareness. You may wish to explore your past experiences concerning a present problem or objective. If, for instance, you are faced with problems in your personal relationships, a deeper understanding of your past-life relationships could offer insight and suggest possible solutions. Or if you are experiencing conflict regarding a career decision, awareness of your past-life career experiences could be an invaluable source of occupational information.

Step 2: Trance Induction by Hand Levitation. Having formulated your objectives, settle back into a comfortable, reclining position, with your legs uncrossed and your hands resting on your thighs. With your eyes closed, mentally scan your body from your head downward, releasing all tension as you go. Upon completing the scan, take a few deep breaths, exhaling slowly. Develop a comfortable, rhythmic breathing pattern, counting backward with each breath from ten to one.

Upon completing the counting, continue breathing rhythmically as you focus your full attention on your hands resting on your thighs. Note specific sensations, such as warmth, tingling, numbness, and the slight pressure of your hands on your thighs. After a few moments of concentration, center your full attention on your right hand and imagine it becoming weightless. Imagine a gentle force under your hand, slowly pushing it upward toward your forehead.

As your hand rises gently, give yourself permission to enter deep hypnosis, and then, to leave your body. With your hand steadily rising, affirm:

When my hand touches my forehead, I will enter a deep hypnotic trance. Upon relaxing my hand and allowing it to return slowly to my thigh, hypnosis will give way to the out-of-body state. Upon leaving my body, I will be fully conscious, safe, and secure. I will be enveloped and protected by the powerful energies and guiding forces of higher cosmic planes. I will return to my body at any moment simply by deciding to do so. Upon returning to my body, I will exit hypnosis simply by counting from one to five.

Allow plenty of time for your hand to levitate until it touches your forehead, then affirm:

I am now in hypnosis and prepared to leave my body simply by relaxing my hand and allowing it to slowly resume its original position.

Let your hand now slowly return to its original position on your thigh.

Step 3: Astral Disengagement. With your hand now resting on your thigh, sense yourself gently leaving your body and rising slowly above it. You can facilitate the disengagement process by envisioning your astral body as a glowing mist lifting quietly from your biological body and remaining suspended over it. Once in the out-of-body state, view your biological body as it remains in a passive state of rest. Sense the powerful radiance enveloping your total being, and affirm:

> *I am now outside my physical body, fully enveloped by pure, radiant cosmic energy. The radiance enveloping my astral being extends to my biological body, protecting and energizing it as I travel to higher astral planes. The highest realms of the cosmos are now receptive to my interaction.*

Step 4: Cosmic Ascension. At this crucial stage of the process, our goals are twofold: first, to ascend to the realm of the cosmic archives, known for its bright hub of light and sweeping swirls of radiant color—and second, to access cosmic sources of past-life experiences. Cosmic ascension is typically accompanied by awareness of specialized astral guides who are almost always enveloped in luminous violet energy. The presence of these guides is invoked by affirmations of your intent to ascend astrally and acquire relevant past-life knowledge. Suggested affirmations include the following:

> *I am now prepared to ascend to the realm of the cosmic archives in my efforts to gain new insight and knowledge concerning my past. I now invoke the empowering presence of astral guides who will be my constant companions throughout this experience.*

The ascension experience is typically characterized by sensations of being gently carried forward—first through darkness, and then into a radiant, fluid-like dimension of varying coloration. Certain dimensions appear as planes of color with many concentrations of light; others emerge as light-filled corridors or channels of energy. During ascension, awareness of time and space is often replaced by a raised state of cosmic awareness, which spontaneously directs our consciousness toward the archival center of cosmic knowledge.

As ascension progresses, you will recognize in the distance a magnificent hub of light with outward spirals of multicolored lights. This luminous core of cosmic energy emits an endless radiance which manifests the creative power of the cosmos. Once in the hub's field of influence, you will experience its gentle attraction drawing you slowly into its central region. Our approach to the cosmic core is invariably accompanied by an expanded awareness of our one-ness with the universe. No longer simply an astral traveler, we are now an integral part of the cosmos, interconnected and interacting with its limitless knowledge and power.

Upon entering the bright cosmic hub, you will notice the sur-rounding multicolored lights forming a great wall of many side-by-side vertical frames, within which your past unfolds in chronological order, from your pre-incarnation existence to your present incarna-tion. Each vertical frame represents a significant period of your past, with the first frame depicting a record of your pre-incarnate exis-tence, and each successive frame depicting either a lifetime or a dis-carnate interval between lives. Pictured in each frame is the progression of your growth, beginning at the bottom of the frame and culminating at the top. The last frame, which is incomplete, is the record your present lifetime.

As your past unfolds before you in these vertical frames, you will notice the continuity and common themes of your life. The total cosmic span of your past, including each cosmic frame and its com-plete contents, is now at your command.

Commanding your attention are certain highlighted contents that represent significant events or turning points in your evolution. Guided by the higher wisdom of the cosmos, you can allow the frames to progressively unfold, or you can arrest certain frames, download specific contents, including those highlighted, and focus on their empowering relevance.

It is important to emphasize the confidential nature of cosmic archives. The cosmic records of each individual are available to that individual alone.

Step 5: Astral Return. To end the ascension experience, affirm your intent to return to your physical body, which is resting com-fortably at a distance. Sense again the presence of your escorting guides, who are now poised to accompany your return and guide your re-entry. Upon re-engaging your physical body, the hypnotic trance will be spontaneously resumed.

Step 6: Resolution and Conclusion. Allow the hypnotic trance to continue as you reflect briefly on the ascension experience, then affirm:

*Upon ending this trance state by counting from one to five, I will
have immediate and full recall of all that I experienced during my
out-of-body ascension. I will understand the significance of this
experience, and use the knowledge gained from it to enrich and
empower my life.*

As you count from one to five, intersperse your counting with
suggestions of increased wakefulness.

Conclude the procedure by further reflecting on the ascension
experience and contemplating its relevance. Give particular attention to the events that commanded your attention, and the common
threads that characterized your past-life history.

Day Six

Objective: *To experience the therapeutic benefits of OBEs.*

Day six in our plan introduces *Astral Plane Therapy,* which is based on the
concept that simply experiencing the higher astral planes is inherently
therapeutic. Even in the absence of clearly formulated goals, this strategy
is energizing and empowering and spontaneously generates positive feelings of security and self-worth. It can be structured, however, to achieve
highly specific therapy goals—such as overcoming depression, reducing
anxiety, and breaking unwanted habits. In the group therapy setting, this
procedure has been highly effective in generating positive interactions
and building productive relationships.

A comfortable, reclining position is recommend for Astral Plane Therapy, which requires approximately one hour in a setting free of distractions. Here is the procedure:

Step 1: Body Scan. With your eyes closed, mentally scan your
body while relaxing each muscle, beginning at your forehead and
progressing downward. When the scan is complete and your body
is completely relaxed, focus your full attention on your breathing.
Continue focusing on your breathing until it develops a slow,
rhythmic pattern.

Step 2: Out-of-Body Induction. With your body now fully relaxed,
envision yourself so liberated from the pressures of life that you begin
to drift gently upward like a white vapor, away from your physical

body, leaving all your cares behind. Notice the sense of freedom and wondrous release from your body, at rest below you.

Step 3: Affirmation. As you remain suspended over your body and enveloped in radiant light, affirm: *I am now balanced, energized, and at peace with myself and the universe.* Mentally invoke the power of higher astral planes, and notice that colorful concentrations of pure cosmic energy are slowly emerging from a distance and surrounding your astral body. Think of each color as representing a particular cosmic resource, such as green for good health, blue for tranquillity, and yellow for enlightenment. Allow each colorful concentration to permeate your entire being. Notice the forceful infusion of positive energy. Allow yourself to remain in this quiet, unencumbered state until your entire being is saturated with power.

Step 4: Re-engagement and Re-affirmation. Gently re-engage your physical body by slowly descending and settling into it. Before opening your eyes, focus again on your breathing, then affirm, *I am now fully infused with abundant energy and power.*

Day Seven

Objective: *To access new growth resources by interacting with the higher astral planes.*

Our seven-day plan concludes with *Astral Outsourcing,* which is designed to access multiple astral planes and activate their empowerment resources. Through this procedure, we can actively engage various astral planes and interact with evolving discarnates as well as advanced astral entities, including angels, guides, teachers, and other specialized growth facilitators. This procedure empowers us to gather the astral resources relevant to our present growth. Here is the procedure:

Step 1: Outsourcing preliminaries. Approximately one hour should be allowed for Astral Outsourcing, during which there must be no distractions. Assume a reclining position with your legs uncrossed and your arms resting comfortably at your sides. To begin the procedure, specify your goals, then relax your physical body using cognitive techniques such as body scan, deep breathing, and peaceful mental imagery. Once your body is fully relaxed, introduce affirmations to facilitate travel and empowering interactions. For this procedure, saying the affirmations aloud seems to make them more effective. Recommended affirmations are:

I am surrounded by peace and tranquillity as I travel out-of-body to experience the highest realms of spiritual reality. I am sheltered and protected by caring guides, who will be my constant companions throughout this experience. The limitless wisdom and power of the cosmos await my search and welcome my interaction.

Step 2: Outsourcing Induction. To induce the out-of-body state, close your eyes and envision your physical body at rest. Take as much time as you need to form a clear image of your physical body, then envision your astral double as a light form bearing your consciousness, rising gently upward and away. Once you reach a full sense of separation from your physical body, mentally reaffirm your intent to explore distant astral realms and engage the presence of accompanying astral guides. Use imagery of distant planes and astral guides to reinforce your affirmations. At this point in the procedure, you will likely experience the unmistakable presence of astral guides as they ascend with you toward the spiritual planes. Upon reaching the spiritual dimension, many travelers experience wonder at the breaking of the cosmic energy barrier and the awesome emergence of the astral realm. Entrance into that splendid realm is almost always accompanied by awareness of multiple colors and a magnificent infusion of cosmic energy, along with a sense of belonging and oneness with the universe.

Step 3: Multi-Colored Outsourcing. At this step, the infusion of cosmic energy continues as you engage the multi-colored astral plane. If you have practiced Past-Life Excursion, or other regression procedures that explore life between lives, you will immediately recognize this familiar zone, in which teachers, guides, angels, and other ministering entities appear as warm, nurturing friends. Telepathy is the communication mode, and pure love characterizes every empowering interaction. Discarnates, some of whom are familiar, are typically present in indescribably beautiful surroundings.

The major resource of the multi-colored plane is cosmic love, the essential element in our spiritual evolution. You can infuse yourself with pure cosmic love simply by lingering in this dimension and interacting with its growth facilitators. Cosmic love is the most powerful force in the universe. It empowers our total being—mentally, physically, and spiritually—with positive energy and vitality. A full infusion of cosmic love provides the basic foundation required for outsourcing the more highly specialized planes in the cosmos.

Although deeply personal interactions with discarnates can occur while outsourcing other planes, they often unfold at this level. Common examples are joyful reunions with the departed, including relatives, friends, and animals. These interactions are invariably empowering for all involved.

Step 4: Specialized Outsourcing. At this point in the procedure, you can choose to conclude the out-sourcing experience by going directly to Step 5, or you can continue out-sourcing by tapping into the more specific resources of other planes through *Specialized Outsourcing.* Numerous specialized planes, each with a predominate color that signifies its specialty, are available for outsourcing. The pure white energy realm is experienced by astral travelers only indirectly, as a distant source of energy and coloration for all planes.

The specialized planes most frequently experienced during outsourcing are violet, blue, green, yellow, orange, and red. Each plane has its own resources, growth frequencies, and specialized growth facilitators. Ministering guides pass freely among the various planes, and often escort out-of-body travelers from plane to plane. Visits among different planes can be spontaneous or selected by personal choice, in collaboration with astral guides.

Outsourcing the Violet Plane

The astral planes of violet, which are among the most brilliant in the cosmos, are associated with spiritual enlightenment and actualization. They are usually situated near the brilliant white light at the center of the celestial cosmos. Interactions with violet planes and their growth facilitators are enlightening and inspiring. They can answer questions concerning the purpose of our lives and the meaning of our existence—past, present, and future. They can connect us to the highest power in the cosmos. They can balance our lives and bring us into a state of oneness with all that exists. All our temporal dilemmas and anxieties succumb to the empowering interactions that take place on this unique plane—hopelessness and despair are replaced by faith and inner peace.

Outsourcing the Blue Plane

The blue planes, which are numerous, are valued for their balancing and attuning qualities. The blue plane is universally attracting, and many travelers are drawn to it. You can voluntarily enter the blue plane simply by focusing on and communicating your intent to the ministering guides who are always present during outsourcing. Travelers who need balance and harmony in their lives will benefit particularly from interactions with this plane.

Outsourcing the Green Plane

The green astral planes are known primarily for their mental, spiritual, and physical healing powers. When bathed in the energies of this plane, the astral body becomes revitalized and empowered to transport healing energy to the physical body at rest in its distant physical setting. The result can be a powerful infusion of mental, spiritual, and physical rejuvenation.

To negotiate the green plane, focus your awareness on its gravitation-like force and give yourself permission to be drawn further into its field. Entry into the plane is usually gradual, with progressive infusions of vitality and rejuvenation. Upon fully engaging with this plane, most travelers experience a peak infusion of healing warmth—which can, in turn, be transported simply by intent back to the physical body.

Outsourcing the Yellow Plane

The yellow astral planes are important to our personal empowerment because of their capacity to promote learning and intellectual growth. Maximizing the empowering effects of the yellow plane, however, usually requires a series of out-of-body travels that recognize the plane's various energies and our capacity to tap into them. Over time, outsourcing this plane can literally raise the IQ.

Outsourcing the Orange Plane

Motivation and nurturance are the specialties of the orange astral planes. The orange planes typically function primarily as passageways or gateways to other planes. Typically situated between the yellow and green planes, they combine the frequencies of both, to motivate learning and nurture healthful change. The benefits of outsourcing all the other specialized planes are spontaneously nurtured through experiencing the energies of the orange plane.

Outsourcing the Red Plane

The red plane is one of the most intensely powerful planes in the cosmos. This plane's primary function is short-term intervention and remediation, under the auspices of highly trained astral specialists. Out-of-body travelers who enter the red plane usually experience a searching review of their lives, including fleeting glimpses of important past incarnations. Although astral outsourcing on this plane is brief, it can uncover critical growth blockages and identify effective ways of overcoming them.

Following interaction with the red plane, outsourcing the green plane to infuse the mind, body, and spirit with healing energy is recommended.

Step 5: Outsourcing Return and Conclusion. Astral return to the biological body begins with the conscious intent to end outsourcing, followed by the simple affirmation: *I am now ready to return to my physical body.* Attention is then focused on the physical body at rest in its familiar environment, followed by awareness of accompanying guides and a gentle re-entry. Various physical sensations signal the completion of full astral/biological re-engagement.

Astral outsourcing is concluded by a brief period of contemplation, followed by affirmations to reinforce the empowering effects of the experience. Examples are:

I am at my peak mentally, physically, and spiritually. I am aware of my potentials, and I am empowered to develop them. I am enveloped in peace and tranquillity. My life is filled with love and joy. I believe in myself and the power within me. I am attuned to the highest powers of the cosmos.

These concluding statements can be supplemented by globally relevant affirmations, such as:

I am committed to helping others and making the planet a better place. I will use my resources to prevent human and animal suffering and abuse. I will work toward ending hunger and poverty, wherever they are found in the world. I will help promote world peace.

Our seven-day plan now complete, we have taken a major step toward enriching our lives with new meaning and power. Given the procedures included in this plan, along with those presented throughout this book, we now have command of new skills that can be used whenever needed to probe the boundless sources of power, from the innermost self to the most distant reaches of the cosmos. We can activate new growth processes and accelerate the development of our highest potentials. We can achieve our loftiest goals while enriching our lives with new insight and fulfillment. We can contribute to the growth of others and make the planet a better place for all who follow us.

12

Conclusion

Truth is on the march, and nothing can stop it now.

Emile Zola, *"J'accuse"*

THE MESSAGE OF OBEs is clear: Each of us is an indestructible force in the universe, whose destiny is both permanence and greatness. Whatever the nature of the out-of-body experience, and wherever we are in our personal growth spiral, OBEs reveal our incomparable worth as human beings, and our capacity to achieve our highest dreams.

OBEs are cosmic gifts. They teach us about ourselves and the beauty of our existence in the universe. They are inexhaustible sources of enlightenment and power. They give inspiration in the face of disappointments and setbacks. They turn problems into exciting growth opportunities, and dissolve the barriers that all too often thwart our evolution. They connect each of us to the greatest teachers and therapists in the cosmos. They sustain us in times of trouble, and comfort us when we are in pain. They lift us above the commonplace, and motivate us to press forward with new hope and joy. They guide us through the darkness, and help us master the fine art of abundant living.

Through OBEs, the unsearchable riches of the cosmos are at our fingertips. Whether we wish to probe the past, explore the present, or access the future, we now have the technology—and through practice we can master it to accelerate our personal development and raise the collective consciousness of the planet. We can induce the out-of-body state, and either focus it on designated goals, or simply allow it to unfold effortlessly, as an expression of our higher self. We can experience the deepest part of ourselves, and tap into the highest planes of the cosmos.

In our study of OBEs throughout this book, we have examined both the process and the product of our personal evolution—and we have found that the ultimate responsibility for both rests within ourselves. We may have made many important discoveries, and possibly reached certain critical decisions, about the meaning of our existence in the cosmos. We may have found some important solutions or achieved an important personal goal—but always, we found ourselves involved in the process. And perhaps that is the greatest and most empowering reward of all.

Glossary

age regression: A phenomenon in which the individual, typically during hypnosis, recalls or re-experiences past experiences lost to present memory. See *past-life regression*.

Astral Blue Beltway: The fluid stream of psychic energy used to convey telepathic messages in the Astral Telepathy System.

astral body: The extra-biological part of our being, which exists as a conscious, intelligent, and indestructible entity.

Astral Flow: A procedure designed to arrest sleep and induce out-of-body travel to designated destinations.

astral genotype: The unique cosmic structure underlying each person's individuality as a conscious entity.

Astral Outsourcing: A procedure designed to acquire outer growth resources available only through out-of-body interactions with higher astral planes.

181

Astral PK: A procedure designed to muster PK resources during the out-of-body state, and focus them on specific health or fitness goals.

Astral Plane Therapy: A psychotherapy procedure based on the concept that the out-of-body experience is inherently therapeutic.

Astral Polarization: An OBEs induction strategy designed to create a polarized state between the astral and biological bodies and a slow separation of the two.

astral projection: A phenomenon in which the astral body disengages from the biological body to consciously experience distant realities. See *out-of-body experiences (OBEs)*.

Astral Regression Therapy: A psychotherapy procedure structured specifically to extinguish deep-seated fears by traveling out-of-body to re-experience their origins.

Astral Surfing: An out-of-body induction procedure designed to facilitate out-of-body astral scanning of multiple planes.

Astral Sweep: A procedure designed to induce out-of-body clairvoyant scanning.

Astral Telepathy System (ATS): A nine-step out-of-body induction and telepathic sending system.

Astral Walk: An out-of-body induction procedure that introduces out-of-body walking as a figurative, multi-directional phenomenon.

Astral Walk-Out: In Astral Walk, a stage in which the astral body disengages the biological body. See *Astral Walk*.

ATS: See *Astral Telepathy System (ATS)*.

bi-location: During the out-of-body state, the capacity of consciousness to simultaneously engage itself in two realities.

biological genotype: The genetic make-up of our biological being.

broken-corona effect: In electrophotography, the phenomenon in which the electromagnetic pattern around the fingerpad separates into two parts during the out-of-body state. See *electrophotography*.

Chalice of Power: In the PK Pool of Power, a procedure used to take water from the PK astral pool and pour it over the astral body. See *PK Pool of Power*.

clairvoyance: Psychic insight concerning distant, unseen realities.

Clairvoyant Sweeping: In Astral Sweep, a liberation of the clairvoyant faculty to probe other realities. See *Astral Sweep*.

continuum of attentiveness: A phenomenon characterizing the liberated discarnate state, in which command of past experiences exists on a need-to-know basis.

continuum of awareness: A phenomenon characterizing the typical incarnate state of constricted memory.

corona-discharge photography: See *electrophotography*.

cosmic actualization: The full realization of personal growth potentials related to past-life experiences.

cosmic archives: The comprehensive records of the cosmos, which include our personal archives.

Cosmic Exposé: A strategy designed to activate out-of-body precognition by focusing on external, cosmic sources of precognition.

cosmic illumination: Raised awareness of the cosmic scheme of our existence, accompanied by increased knowledge of our higher self. See *cosmic actualization*.

cosmic life force: The energizing foundation of all reality, both tangible and intangible.

cosmic map: In Past-Life Excursion, a chart of the orbs and lines representing elements of our past, including pre-incarnate, incarnate, and discarnate experiences. See *Past-Life Excursion.*

Crystalline Sphere Technique: A psychotherapy technique designed to explore past-life influences and extinguish fears associated with unresolved past-life trauma.

discarnate compensation: In discarnate development, the capacity of astral teachers and other growth specialists to make up for a deficiency in a given individual's accumulated incarnate resources.

discarnate history: A record of one's personal existence in the discarnate realm between past lifetimes and following one's final incarnation.

discarnate illumination: Raised awareness and understanding of past-life influences on our present growth and enlightenment.

electrophotography: A photographic procedure that records the electromagnetic energy patterns surrounding the physical body. Also known as corona-discharge photography or Kirlian photography.

ESP: See *extrasensory perception.*

expansive consciousness: An out-of-body state in which personal identity remains intact with acute awareness of one's own being as an independent entity.

extrasensory perception (ESP): The knowledge of, or response to, events, conditions, and situations known independently of sensory mechanisms or processes.

hand levitation: A hypnotic induction procedure in which the hand levitates to induce the trance state.

hypnosis: An altered state of consciousness in which concentration is focused and receptivity to suggestion is heightened.

In-Body Travel: An OBEs practice exercise involving centering attention on isolated body parts and inducing new physical sensations.

incarnate history: A record of one's past incarnations on this earth plane.

Kirlian photography: See *electrophotography*.

materialization: A tangible representation of astral energy, in which thoughts, other intangibles, or, in some instances, distant tangibles assume a physical presence, often spontaneously.

Mirror Image: An induction procedure utilizing a mirror to facilitate astral disengagement from the biological body.

Moon View: An out-of-body experience preparatory exercise which involves focusing on the moon and imagining visiting it.

multi-location: The capacity of consciousness in the out-of-body state to simultaneously engage itself in multiple realities. See *bi-location*.

NDEs: See *near-death experiences (NDEs)*.

near-death experiences (NDEs): Experiences in which death appears imminent, often accompanied by a sense of separation of consciousness from the biological body.

OBEs: See *out-of-body experiences (OBEs)*.

OBEs Levitation: An induction procedure using sensations of physical weightlessness to facilitate astral disengagement.

Out-of-body Aura Massage: In the PK Channeling strategy, the aura surrounding the physical body of the receiving subject is massaged. See *PK Channeling*.

out-of-body clairvoyance: The psychic perception of present realities while in the out-of-body state.

out-of-body experiences (OBEs): States of awareness in which one's extrabiological part as a conscious, intelligent entity disengages from one's physiology to experience reality independent of the biological body. See *astral projection*.

out-of-body precognition: The psychic perception of future events while in the out-of-body state.

out-of-body psychokinesis: The psychic capacity while in the out-of-body state to influence matter.

out-of-body telepathy: Mind-to-mind communication while either sender or receiver, or both, are in the out-of-body state.

Past-Life Ascent: A procedure that combines hypnosis and the out-of-body state to retrieve past-life experiences and glean empowering knowledge from them.

Past-Life Excursion: A procedure designed to spontaneously retrieve past-life experiences that are presently relevant.

past-life journal: A running record of past-life experiences retrieved through Past-Life Ascent. See *Past-Life Ascent*.

past-life regression: A phenomenon in which past-life experiences can be retrieved, and in some instances re-experienced, typically during hypnosis.

Personal Exposé: A strategy designed to activate out-of-body precognition by focusing on the internal sources of precognitive awareness.

PK: See *psychokinesis (PK)*.

PK Channeling: An out-of-body procedure designed to access the healing resources of higher planes and transfer them to the physical body.

PK Pool of Power: A procedure designed to promote health and fitness through out-of-body psychokinesis.

precognition: The psychic awareness of future events.

pre-incarnate history: A record of one's personal existence prior to one's first incarnation.

Principle of continuity: The view that growth is a never-ending process.

Principle of cumulative effects: The view that we are, at any given moment, the totality of all our previous personal experiences.

psychokinesis (PK): The capacity of the mind to influence objects, events, and processes in the absence of intervening physical energy or instrumentation.

reincarnation: A developmental phenomenon based on the concept of multiple past lives and the indestructible nature of consciousness.

reincarnation reversal: A past-life role, characteristic, or activity is reversed in a later life.

remote-image phenomenon: In electrophotography, a point or small cluster occurring in a remote area outside the normal region of corona-discharge activity.

retrocognition: Psychic awareness of the past.

Sexual Interchange Strategy: A form of out-of-body sexual interaction involving temporary gender reversal.

silver cord: An energy system connecting the astral body to the biological body during the out-of-body state.

telepathy: Mind-to-mind communication.

Index

☾ LOOK FOR THE CRESCENT MOON

Llewellyn publishes hundreds of books on your favorite subjects! To get these exciting books, including the ones on the following pages, check your local bookstore or order them directly from Llewellyn.

ORDER BY PHONE
- Call toll-free within the U.S. and Canada, 1-800-THE MOON
- In Minnesota, call (612) 291-1970
- We accept VISA, MasterCard, and American Express

ORDER BY MAIL
- Send the full price of your order (MN residents add 7% sales tax) in U.S. funds, plus postage & handling to:

  Llewellyn Worldwide
  P.O. Box 64383, Dept. K636-X
  St. Paul, MN 55164–0383, U.S.A.

POSTAGE & HANDLING
(For the U.S., Canada, and Mexico)
- $4.00 for orders $15.00 and under
- $5.00 for orders over $15.00
- No charge for orders over $100.00

We ship UPS in the continental United States. We ship standard mail to P.O. boxes. Orders shipped to Alaska, Hawaii, The Virgin Islands, and Puerto Rico are sent first-class mail. Orders shipped to Canada and Mexico are sent surface mail.

International orders: Airmail—add freight equal to price of each book to the total price of order, plus $5.00 for each non-book item (audio tapes, etc.).

Surface mail—Add $1.00 per item.

Allow 4–6 weeks for delivery on all orders.
Postage and handling rates subject to change.

DISCOUNTS
We offer a 20% discount to group leaders or agents. You must order a minimum of 5 copies of the same book to get our special quantity price.

Visit our web site at www.llewellyn.com for more information.

PSYCHIC EMPOWERMENT
A 7-Day Plan for Self-Development

Joe H. Slate, Ph.D.

Use 100% of your mind power in just one week! You've heard it before: each of us is filled with an abundance of untapped power—yet we only use one-tenth of its potential. Now a clinical psychologist and famed researcher in parapsychology shows you how to probe your mind's psychic faculties and manifest your capacity to access the higher planes of the mind.

The psychic experience validates your true nature and connects you to your inner knowing. Dr. Slate reveals the life-changing nature of psychic phenomena—including telepathy, out-of-body experiences and automatic writing. At the same time, he shows you how to develop a host of psychic abilities including psychokinesis, crystal gazing, and table tilting.

The final section of the book outlines his accelerated 7-Day Psychic Development Plan through which you can unleash your innate power and wisdom without further delay.

1-56718-635-1, 6 x 9, 256 pp., softcover $12.95

To order, call 1-800-THE-MOON
Prices subject to change without notice

PSYCHIC EMPOWERMENT
FOR HEALTH AND FITNESS

Joe H. Slate, Ph.D.

Can you really "program" your mind during sleep for positive health results the next day? Yes! In the last decade we have learned more about our mental, physical, and spiritual nature than in the past century. In this quest for knowledge we have discovered that our minds hold the power to directly affect our physical health. In fact, the ability of the mind to access the highest dimensions of reality can actually facilitate weight loss, self-control, and, ultimately, optimal fitness.

Psychic Empowerment for Health and Fitness walks you through a program of psychic exercises that actually can transform your physical body. Your upward spiral to feeling great will begin quickly with Dr. Slate's structured 7-Day Plan for Health & Fitness. You'll tap your mind's deep power and soon experience a relief from stress and anxiety. Find out why psychic protection procedures really are necessary to your health. See for yourself how psychokinesis (PK) and crystals can energize and heal our earth and all her populations. Effect an environmental clearing or a tree power interfusion. The actions you take based on this book will not only benefit you, but our planet as well.

1-56718-634-3, 256 pp., 6 x 9, softcover $12.95

PSYCHIC DEVELOPMENT FOR BEGINNERS

An Easy Guide to Releasing and DevelopingYour Psychic Abilities
William Hewitt

Psychic Development for Beginners provides detailed instruction on developing your sixth sense, or psychic ability. Improve your sense of worth, your sense of responsibility and therefore your ability to make a difference in the world. Innovative exercises like "The Skyscraper" allow beginning students of psychic development to quickly realize personal and material gain through their own natural talent.

Benefits range from the practical to spiritual. Find a parking space anywhere, handle a difficult salesperson, choose a compatible partner, and even access different time periods! Practice psychic healing on pets or humans—and be pleasantly surprised by your results. Use psychic commands to prevent dozing while driving. Preview out-of-body travel, cosmic consciousness and other alternative realities. Instruction in *Psychic Development for Beginners* is supported by personal anecdotes, 44 psychic development exercises, and 28 related psychic case studies to help students gain a comprehensive understanding of the psychic realm.

1-56718-360-3, 5¼ x 8, 216 pp., softcover $9.95

AURA READING
FOR BEGINNERS
Develop Your Psychic Awareness for
Health & Success
Richard Webster

When you lose your temper, don't be surprised if a dirty red haze suddenly appears around you. If you do something magnanimous, your aura will expand. Now you can learn to see the energy that emanates off yourself and other people through the proven methods taught by Richard Webster in his psychic training classes.

Learn to feel the aura, see the colors in it, and interpret what those colors mean. Explore the chakra system, and how to restore balance to chakras that are over- or under-stimulated. Then you can begin to imprint your desires into your aura to attract what you want in your life.

These proven methods for seeing the aura will help you:
- Interpret the meanings of colors in the aura
- Find a career that is best suited for you
- Relate better to the people you meet and deal with
- Enjoy excellent health
- Discover areas of your life that you need to work on
- Make aura portraits with pastels or colored pencils
- Discover the signs of impending ill health, drug abuse, and pain
- Change the state of your aura and stimulate specific chakras through music, crystals, color
- See what the next few weeks or months are going to be like for you

1-56718-798-6, 5 3/16 x 8, 208 pp., illus. $7.95

SELF-HYPNOSIS
FOR A BETTER LIFE

William W. Hewitt

The sound of your own voice is an incredibly powerful tool for speaking to and reprogramming your subconscious. Now, for the first time, you can select your own self-hypnosis script and record it yourself. *Self-Hypnosis for a Better Life* gives the exact wording for 23 unique situations that can be successfully handled with self-hypnosis. Each script is complete in itself and only takes 30 minutes to record. You simply read the script aloud into a tape recorder, then replay the finished tape back to yourself and reap the rewards of self-hypnosis!

Whether you want to eradicate negativity from your life, attract a special romantic partner, solve a problem, be more successful at work, or simply relax, you will find a number of tapes to suit your needs. Become your own hypnotherapist as you design your own self-improvement program, and you can make anything happen.

1-56718-358-1, 5 3/16 x 8, 256 pp., illus., softcover $9.95

REINCARNATION: REMEMBERING PAST LIVES

Break Free from Your Past
Genevieve Lewis Paulson &
Stephen J. Paulson

Why is knowledge of your past lives of any value to your present life? Traumatic events from the past can create blocks to your current growth and joys. Attitudes can carry over that hold you back from healthy relationships. Irrational fears with no known cause can sometimes be traced back to events in previous lives.

Reincarnation: Remembering Past Lives shows you how to enter into your own meditative state and access your own experiences and knowledge. Explore your cycles of lives…soul mates and soul relationships…soul families and tribes…the akashic records…genetic influences…the many facets of karma and how to transmute it…the process of evolution…leading past life regressions for others…how to die gracefully…finding your soul teacher…opening to your intuition…and much more.

1-56718-511-8, 5 3/16 x 8, 224 pp., illus., softcover $7.95

MIND MAGIC KIT

Dr. Jonn Mumford
(Swami Anandakapila Saraswati)

The *Mind Magic Kit* is a dynamic program that gives you the ultimate combination of stress-management tools: fractional relaxation and autogenic temperature control. The kit includes an audio cassette, instruction book and a hand-held biofeedback thermometer with which to gauge your progress. Side one of the tape, "Fractional relaxation," guides you through a progressive relaxation that eliminates mental tension and cultivates life-affirming states of mind. Side two of the tape, "Autogenic Training," is your gateway to thermal biofeedback (control of circulation in the hands and feet), voluntary control of your autonomic nervous system and meditation. It uses a simple trigger word as a mantra, which when silently repeated will lead you into the interior depths of yourself. Practice the autogenic temperature control techniques provided in this kit and …

- Learn the secret key code word that will move you quickly into deep meditative states
- Alleviate psychosomatic illness
- Increase secretion of the pineal hormone melatonin to reverse aging, fight cancer and rejuvenate energy
- Learn to master anxiety, nervousness, migraines, Raynaud's disease, and insomnia
- Improve your concentration skills, your relaxation response, and your ability to change your attitudes

1-56718-475-8, Boxed kit: audiotape; 5³⁄16 x 8, 96-pp. booklet; biofeedback thermometer $15.95

To order, call 1-800-THE-MOON
Prices subject to change without notice